The Authors

WILLIAM F. MARTIN served as U.S. Deputy Secretary of Energy, Executive Secretary of the National Security Council in the White House, and Special Assistant to President Ronald Reagan. In 1992, he was Executive Director of the Republican Party National Platform Committee. During the second oil crisis, Mr. Martin was Special Assistant to the Executive Director of the International Energy Agency, Ulf Lantzke. He also held positions in the Department of State and MIT's Workshop on Alternative Energy Strategies headed by Carroll L. Wilson. Today, he is Chairman of Washington Policy and Analysis, Inc., an international energy consulting firm. He holds degrees from the University of Pennsylvania and MIT. Mr. Martin is a member of the Board of the World Resources Institute, and a member of the Council on Foreign Relations, New York.

RYUKICHI IMAI is Professor of Social Sciences at Kyorin University Graduate School; a visiting Professor at Sophia University; and a Distinguished Research Fellow at the Institute of International Policy Studies in Tokyo. Previously, he served as Japan's Ambassador to the Conference on Disarmament in Geneva, to Kuwait, and to Mexico. Before joining the Ministry of Foreign Affairs, he was General Manager for Engineering at the Japan Atomic Power Company. He holds degrees from the University of Tokyo (including a Ph.D. in nuclear engineering), the Fletcher School of Law and Diplomacy, and Harvard. His books include: *Science and Nation, Nuclear Energy and Nuclear Proliferation* (with Henry Rowen), *Nuclear Disarmament, and Post-Cold War Nuclear Weapons Management.*

HELGA STEEG was the Executive Director of the International Energy Agency from 1984 to 1994. Before joining the International Energy Agency, she held several senior positions with the Federal Republic of Germany's Economic Ministry in the fields of money, credit, trade, and economics. From 1973 to 1984, she was the Director General (Ministerialdirektor) of the Department of Foreign Economic Policy. From 1964 to 1967, she was the German Alternate Executive Director of the World Bank. Today, she teaches International Energy Policy at the Ruhr-University Bochum. Ms. Steeg received her training in the fields of international law and economics at the Universities of Bonn and Lausanne.

Maintaining Energy Security in a Global Context

A Report to
The Trilateral Commission

Authors: William F. Martin
Chairman, Washington Policy and Analysis, Inc.;
former U.S. Deputy Secretary of Energy

Ryukichi Imai
Distinguished Research Fellow, Institute for
International Policy Studies, Tokyo;
former Japanese Ambassador to Kuwait, Mexico
and the Conference on Disarmament in Geneva

Helga Steeg
Former Executive Director,
International Energy Agency

published by
The Trilateral Commission
New York, Paris and Tokyo
September 1996

Library of Congress Cataloging-in-Publication Data

Martin, William Flynn, 1950-

Maintaining Energy Security in a Global Context: a report to the
    Trilateral Commission/by William F. Martin, Ryukichi Imai, Helga
    Steeg
        p. cm. — (The Triangle papers: 48)
    Includes bibliographical references

ISBN 0-930503-73-2
1. Energy policy. 2. Petroleum industry and trade—Government
policy. 3. Nuclear industry. 4. Energy industries—Environmental
aspects. I. Imai, Ryukichi, 1929-   . II. Steeg, Helga.
III. Trilateral Commission. IV. Title. V. Series.
HD9502.A2M3515   1996
333.79—dc20

                                                        96-28121
                                                            CIP
Manufactured in the United States of America

THE TRILATERAL COMMISSION

345 East 46th Street   c/o Japan Center for   35, avenue de Friedland
New York, NY 10017   International Exchange   75008 Paris, France
                            4-9-17 Minami-Azabu
                            Minato-ku
                            Tokyo, Japan

The Trilateral Process

The report which follows is the joint responsibility of three authors, with William Martin serving as lead author. Although only the authors are responsible for the analyses and conclusions, they have been aided in their work by many others. The authors would like to express particular appreciation to Antony Barton (a Canadian citizen), Director of Research at Washington Policy and Analysis, who carried out the fresh research required for the preparation of this report and served as rapporteur during the study. Amelia Barton of Washington Policy and Analysis assisted Mr. Martin with the Global Energy Supply and Demand Model and designed most of the visuals in the report. The authors would also like to express appreciation to Charles Heck, North American Director of the Trilateral Commission, for drafting and editing assistance.

The authors were enlisted and work begun on this report in the late spring and summer of 1995. Martin and Imai met for a preliminary discussion in Washington on September 10, and Steeg and Imai in Berlin on September 16. The first full authors' meeting was on October 10-11 in Tokyo, where Steeg also spoke at the World Energy Conference. Martin had prepared an extensive discussion paper for the Tokyo meeting, in effect a somewhat skeletal first draft of the report. The authors next met in Bonn on January 27-29, 1996, focusing on Martin's next draft and its main themes. The succeeding draft was circulated to Trilateral Commission members in early April and discussed at the Commission's 1996 annual meeting in Vancouver on April 20-22. Final revisions for publication were completed in late July.

As the following list indicates, the authors consulted extensively in the course of their work. Martin's Washington consultations were concentrated in December, January and February—including discussions at the Department of Energy, Central Intelligence Agency, National Security Council, Department of State, World Bank and World Resources Institute, among others. In January he traveled to New Mexico for discussions at the Los Alamos National Laboratory. In February he traveled to Ottawa for consultations with Canadian government officials (both active and former), representatives from private industry, and several Canadian Trilateral Commission members. In March he traveled to Dallas for a discussion of the world energy outlook with several persons on the planning staff of the

Exxon Corporation. In Europe, Steeg talked about the project with former colleagues at the International Energy Agency in Paris in October 1995—a number of persons from the IEA have been most helpful throughout this project. She returned to Paris for consultations on June 11-12, 1996, with French government ministries, Electricité de France, the French Atomic Energy Commission, and the planning staff of Elf Aquitaine. In Germany, all three authors participated in meetings on January 29, 1996, at the Economics Ministry and Deutsche Gesellschaft für Auswärtige Politik. Steeg traveled to London on January 11 and to Rome on January 15 for discussions with government officials, business leaders, energy experts and Trilateral Commission members. Imai's consultations in Japan included a range of persons from government ministries, energy companies and industry associations, universities and research institutes. More specifically, the Committee for Energy Policy Promotion devoted evening meetings to discussion of drafts of the report, and provided valuable advice from the point of view of the private energy sector. The Institute of Energy Economics, where Imai is a research advisor, provided valuable advice and data. Government officials at various levels of the Science and Technology Agency and the Ministry of International Trade and Industry were consulted by Imai in his capacity as Counsellor of the Atomic Energy Commission and as a member of various MITI advisory bodies. The Japan Atomic Industrial Forum provided extensive support regarding the role of nuclear power.

The many persons consulted in the preparation of this report spoke for themselves as individuals and not for any institutions with which they are associated. The authors express their appreciation to them all. They include:

North American Consultations

Edward Arthur, *Project Leader, Nuclear Materials, Los Alamos National Laboratory*

Carl Beard, *Technical Staff Member, Systems Engineering and Integration, Analysis and Assessment Division, Los Alamos National Laboratory*

Robert Berls, Jr., *Special Assistant, Office of the Secretary, U.S. Department of Energy*

Ben Bonk, *National Intelligence Officer for Near East and South Asia, National Intelligence Council, U.S. Central Intelligence Agency*

John Brodman, *Director, Office of International Science and Technology Cooperation, Office of Policy, U.S. Department of Energy*

Zbigniew Brzezinski, *Former National Security Advisor to President Carter; Counselor, Center for Strategic and International Studies*

John Buksa, *Team Leader, Reactor Design and Analysis Group, Los Alamos National Laboratory*

Julie-Ann Canepa, *Earth and Environmental Sciences Directorate, Los Alamos National Laboratory*

Mike Cleland, *Assistant Deputy Minister, Natural Resources Canada*

E. Philip Cockshutt, *Energy Council of Canada*

Gary Coene, *Acting Director of Slavic and Eurasian Analysis, U.S. Central Intelligence Agency*

Richard N. Cooper, *Chairman, National Intelligence Council, U.S. Central Intelligence Agency*

Marshall Crowe, *Former Chairman of the National Energy Board of Canada*

Charles Curtis, *U.S. Deputy Secretary of Energy*

Ian Deans, *Chairperson, Public Service Staff Relations Board of Canada; former Member of Parliament*

John Deutch, *Director, U.S. Central Intelligence Agency*

Peter Dobell, *Director, Parliamentary Centre for Foreign Affairs and Foreign Trade, Ottawa*

Ulrich Dollwet, *Staff Planning Analyst, Corporate Planning Department, Exxon Corporation*

Shaun Donnelly, *Deputy Assistant Secretary for Energy, Sanctions, and Commodities, U.S. Department of State; Chairman of the Standing Group on Long-Term Cooperation, International Energy Agency*

Roger Dower, *Program Director of Climate, Energy, and Pollution Program, World Resources Institute*

Mose Dunning, *Coordinator, Energy and Industry Analysis, Corporate Planning Department, Exxon Corporation*

Joseph Gilling, *Senior Energy Economist, Power Development, Efficiency and Household Fuels, Industry and Energy, The World Bank*

Sue Goff, *Program Manager, Energy Supply and the Environment, Los Alamos National Laboratory*

William Hancox, *Vice President, Strategic Development, Atomic Energy of Canada Limited*

J.P. Harris, *General Manager, Corporate Planning Department, Exxon Corporation*

John Havenstrite, *Senior Planning Advisor, Corporate Strategy Division, Exxon Corporation*

Sigfried Hecker, *Director, Los Alamos National Laboratory*

Michael Houts, *Team Leader, Criticality, Reactor, and Radiation Physics, Nuclear Systems Design and Analysis, Los Alamos National Laboratory*

Jeffrey Hughes, *Assistant to the Deputy Secretary, U.S. Department of Energy*

John Ireland, *Deputy Division Director, Technology and Safety Assessment Division, Los Alamos National Laboratory*

Shirley Jackson, *Chairman, U.S. Nuclear Regulatory Commission*

Colin Kenny, *Vice-Chair, Energy Committee of Canadian Senate*

Robert Krakowski, *Systems Engineering and Integration Group, Technology and Safety Assessment Division, Los Alamos National Laboratory*

Kjell Kristiansen, *Counselor for Energy, Royal Norwegian Embassy, Washington, D.C.*

Joseph Laia, *Director of Environmental Technologies, Los Alamos National Laboratory*

Jonathan Lash, *President, World Resources Institute*

Winston Lord, *U.S. Assistant Secretary of State for East Asian and Pacific Affairs*

Robert Lyman, *Director, Oil Division, Energy Supply Branch, Natural Resources Canada*

James MacKenzie, *Senior Associate of Climate, Energy, and Pollution Program, World Resources Institute*

Wilfred W. Martin Jr., *Independent Oil Producer*

Jessica Tuchman Mathews, *Senior Fellow, Council on Foreign Relations*

Robert McFarlane, *Former National Security Advisor to President Reagan; Chairman of McFarlane Associates, Inc.*

Neil McKeowen, *Energy Security Branch, U.S. Central Intelligence Agency*

Robert S. McNamara, *Former U.S. Secretary of Defense and Past President of the World Bank*

C.W. Myers, *Division Director, Earth and Environmental Sciences Directorate, Los Alamos National Laboratory*

Hazel O'Leary, *U.S. Secretary of Energy*

Willy Olsen, *Vice President, Corporate Planning, Statoil Group, Norway*

Daniel Poneman, *Special Assistant to the President for Non-Proliferation Affairs, U.S. National Security Council*

Mary Preville, *Senior Analyst, International Energy Division, Natural Resources Canada*

William Ramsey, *Deputy Assistant Secretary for Energy, Sanctions and Commodities, U.S. Department of State*

Glenn Rase, *Director of the Office of International Energy Policy, U.S. Department of State*

David Reed, *Staff Planning Advisor, Corporate Planning Department, Exxon Corporation*

Roger Robinson, *Former Chief Economist for the U.S. National Security Council; President, RWR, Inc.*

Yoshiyuki Sakakibara, *Chief Representative, Federation of Electric Power Companies of Japan*

James Schlesinger, *Former U.S. Secretary of Energy; former Director of Central Intelligence and former Secretary of Defense*

Jitendra Shah, *Environment and Natural Resources Division, Asia Technical Department, World Bank*

Richard Stern, *Director, Energy and Industry Department, The World Bank*

Ian Stewart, *Former Canadian Deputy Minister of Energy and of Finance*

Maurice Strong, *Chairman, Earth Council*

Nicholas Swales, *Executive Assistant, Canadian Group, Trilateral Commission*

Mike Telson, *Special Assistant to the Deputy Secretary, U.S. Department of Energy*

Sam Thompson, *Deputy Director-General, Nuclear Energy Agency*

Peter Trinkle, *Senior Advisor, Public Affairs Department, Exxon Corporation*

Enzo Viscusi, *ENI Representative for the Americas*

Ted Williams, *Office of Policy, U.S. Department of Energy*

Peter Witte, *Assistant to the North American Director, Trilateral Commission*

Daniel Yergin, *President, Cambridge Energy Research Associates*

European Consultations

Lisette Andreae, *German Society for Foreign Policy (DGAP), Bonn*

Lord Armstrong, *Director, The R.T.Z. Corporation, London; former Chief Cabinet Secretary to the Prime Minister*

Craig Bamberger, *Legal Counsel, International Energy Agency*

Piero Bassetti, *Chairman, Chamber of Commerce and Industry of Milan; former Member of Italian Chamber of Deputies*

Klaus Becher, *German Society for Foreign Policy (DGAP), Bonn*

Elmar Becker, *Director General, German Federal Economics Ministry; Chairman of the International Energy Agency Governing Board*

Jean Bergougnoux, *Former Director General, Electricité de France (French Electricity Board), Paris; former Chairman, SNCF (French State Railways)*

Ulf Böge, *Director, German Federal Economics Ministry; Deputy Chairman of the International Energy Agency Governing Board*

Marcel Boiteux, *Honorary Chairman, Electricité de France (French Electricity Board), Paris*

Burghard Brock, *German Federal Economics Ministry*

Umberto Cappuzzo, *Member of the Defense Committee, Italian Senate; former Chief of Staff of the Army*

Giuseppe Carta, *Director D.P.S., ENEL, Rome*

Guy Caruso, *Director, Office of Non-Member Countries, International Energy Agency, Paris*

Fausto Cereti, *Chairman and Chief Executive Officer, Alitalia, Rome*

Umberto Colombo, *Chairman, LEAD Europe, Rome; former Italian Minister for Universities, Science and Technology*

Philippe Coste, *Director for European Economic Cooperation, Ministry of Foreign Affairs, Paris*

Yves Cousin, *Executive Vice President Head of the Engineering and Construction Division, Electricité de France (French Electricity Board), Paris*

Wilfried Czernie, *Director, Ruhrgas, Essen*

Thierry Dujardin, *Executive Deputy Director, Division for International Affairs, Commissariat à l'Energie Atomique (French Atomic Energy Commission), Paris*

Tim Eggar, *Member of the British Parliament; Minister for Energy*

Christoph Eitner, *Director, Energy Research Department, German Federal Ministry for Education, Sciences, Research and Technology, Bonn*

Maren Ernst-Vogel, *Mineralölwirtschaftsverband (Oil Industrial Federation), Bonn*

Ugo Farinelli, *Director of Studies, ENEA, Rome*

John Ferriter, *Deputy Executive Director, International Energy Agency, Paris*

Kenneth Friedman, *Head of Energy Technology Policy Division, International Energy Agency, Paris*

Tristan Garel-Jones, *Member of British Parliament; former Minister of State at the Foreign Office (European Affairs)*

Sergio Garribba, *Director of the Energy Department, ENEA, Rome*

Helmut Giesecke, *WSA/Deutscher Industrie and Handelstag (DIHT), Bonn*

John Gilbert, *Member of British Parliament; former Treasury, Transport and Defense Minister; Chairman of John Gilbert and Associates, London*

Roland Götz, *BIOst, Cologne*

Antoine Guéroult, *Deputy Director General for Energy and Raw Materials, Ministry of Industry, Paris*

Marcello Guidi, *Chairman, ISPI, Milan; former Ambassador of Italy*

Erwin Häckel, *German Society for Foreign Policy (DGAP), Bonn*
Wolf Häfele, *Rossendorf Nuclear Research Centre, Germany*
Paul Haseldonckx, *DEMINEX, Essen*
Rolf Hempelmann, *Member of the German Bundestag*
Charles Henderson, *Deputy Secretary for Energy, Department of Trade and Industry, London*
Petra Holtrup, *Jülich Nuclear Research Centre, Germany*
Wolfgang Ischinger, *Director for Political Affairs, German Federal Ministry of Foreign Affairs*
Sir Michael Jenkins, *Vice Chairman, Kleinwort Benson Group, London; former British Ambassador*
Reimut Jochimsen, *President, Central Bank of Northrhine-Westphalia, Düsseldorf; Member of the Central Bank Council of the Deutsche Bundesbank*
Klaus Johanssen, *Energy Department, German Federal Economics Ministry, Bonn*
Hans Kausch, *Head of Non-Member Countries Division, Europe, Middle East and Africa, International Energy Agency, Paris*
Malcolm Keay, *Division Head for Alternative Energy Resources, International Energy Agency, Paris*
Guido Knoff, *Economics Council, CDU Party, Bonn*
Hans Jürgen Koch, *Director, Energy Technology, Research and Development, International Energy Agency, Paris*
Otto Graf Lambsdorff, *Member of the German Bundestag; Honorary Chairman and Chief Economic Spokesman, Free Democratic Party; former Federal Minister of Economy*
Werner Lamby, *President, German Society for Foreign Policy (DGAP), Bonn*
Franz Lamprecht, Energiewirtschaftliche Tagesfragen, *Düsseldorf*
Alan Lee Williams, *Director, The British Atlantic Council; former Member of British Parliament*
Arrigo Levi, *Political Columnist,* Corriere della Sera, *Rome*
Alfonso Limbruno, *Chief Executive Officer, ENEL, Rome*
Jürgen Louis, *VIAG, Bonn*
Carlo Mancini, *Director, International Relations Department, ENEA, Rome*
Claude Mandil, *Director General for Energy and Raw Materials, Ministry of Industry, Paris*
Karl Manshaus, *Secretary-General, Royal Norwegian Ministry of Industry and Energy*
Cesare Merlini, *Chairman of the Executive Committee, Council for the United States and Italy; Chairman, Institute for International Affairs, Rome*

John Mitchell, *Chairman of the Energy and Environmental Programme, The Royal Institute of International Affairs, London*

Gian Marco Moratti, *President, Unione Petrolifera, Rome; President, Saras-Raffinerie Sarde, Milan*

Friedemann Müller, *Stiftung Wissenschaft und Politik, Ebenhausen*

Sir Edwin Nixon, *Deputy Chairman, National Westminster Bank, London*

Sean O'Dell, *Head of Economics, Statistics and Information Systems, International Energy Agency, Paris*

Takashi Okano, *Office of Energy Technology, Research and Development, International Energy Agency, Paris*

Gerhard Ott, *World Energy Council, Essen*

Sir Michael Palliser, *Vice Chairman, Samuel Montagu and Company, London; former British Permanent Under-Secretary of State, Foreign and Commonwealth Office*

Arne Paulson, *Special Assistant to the Deputy Executive Director, International Energy Agency, Paris*

Mark Pellew, *Foreign and Commonwealth Office, London*

Elizabeth Pond, *Writer, Bonn*

Robert Priddle, *Executive Director, International Energy Agency, Paris*

Alexander Rahr, *German Society for Foreign Policy (DGAP), Bonn*

Stefan Reindl, *VEBA, Düsseldorf*

Paul Révay, *European Director, Trilateral Commission*

Alfred Richmann, *Deutscher Industrie und Handelstag (DIHT), Bonn*

Derek Riley, *Chief Economist, Corporate Planning, Elf Aquitaine, Paris*

Ettore Rossini, *Director, General Directorate of Energy, Italian Ministry of Industry, Trade and Crafts*

Walter Sandtner, *Head of Division for Renewable Energies, German Federal Ministry for Education, Sciences, Research and Technology*

Tore Sandvold, *Director-General, Ministry of Industry and Energy, Norway*

François Sauzey, *European Press Officer, Trilateral Commission, Paris*

Reinhard Schlagintweit, *German Society for Foreign Policy (DGAP), Bonn*

Dieter Schmitt, *Professor, University of Essen*

Peter Schutterle, *Secretary General, The Energy Charter Treaty, Brussels*

Giuseppe Sfligiotti, *Chairman, Italian Chemical Society*

Peter Shore, *Member of British Parliament*

Robert Skinner, *Director, Office of Long-Term Energy Policy, International Energy Agency, Paris*

Tohihiro Taniguchi, *Director, Office of Oil Markets and Emergency Preparedness, International Energy Agency, Paris*

Sir Peter Tapsell, *Member of British Parliament*
Michel Valais, *Senior Energy Advisor, Corporate Planning, Elf Aquitaine, Paris*
Yves Vandenboomgaerde, *Executive Deputy Director, Division of Strategy and Evaluation, Commissariat à l'Energie Atomique (French Atomic Energy Commission), Paris*
Ernesto Vellano, *Secretary-Treasurer of the Italian Group of The Trilateral Commission, Turin*
Angelika Volle, *Executive Editor,* Internationale Politik, *German Society for Foreign Policy (DGAP), Bonn*
Karel Vosskühler, *Dutch Embassy, Bonn*
Lord Wakeham, *Former British State Secretary for Energy; Chairman of the Press Complaints Commission, London*
Hans Christian Winkler, *Economics Department, German Federal Ministry of Foreign Affairs*
Giovan Battista Zorzoli, *Chief Executive Officer, T & M*

Japanese Consultations

Kazuya Fujime, *Managing Director, Institute of Energy Economics, Japan*
Wataru Fukazawa, *Director, Japan National Oil Company*
Tomoo Funaki, *Managing Director, Electric Power Development Corporation, Japan*
Shigeo Hiramatsu, *Professor, Kyorin University*
Funao Kifune, *Assistant Professor, Nagoya University*
Kiyoshi Koumura, *Director and General Manager, Industrial Planning, Idemitsu Kosan Company*
Hideo Matsui, *Director, Nuclear Industry, Ministry of International Trade and Industry*
Naoya Minami, *Managing Director, Tokyo Electric Power Company*
Kazuhisa Mori, *Managing Director, Japan Atomic Industrial Forum*
Takayuki Nagano, *Director for International Cooperation, Atomic Energy Bureau, Science and Technology Agency*
Tsuruhiko Nannbu, *Professor, Gakushuin University*
Takashi Nonouchi, *Senior Managing Director, Hitachi; former Director General for Resources and Energy, Ministry of International Trade and Industry*
Kazuo Shimoda, *Managing Director, Committee for Energy Policy Promotion*
Shunji Shimoyama, *Auditor and former Managing Director, Japan Atomic Power Company*

Mamoru Sueda, *Executive Vice President, Committee for Energy Policy Promotion*

Kenichi Suganuma, *Director, International Energy, Ministry of Foreign Affairs*

Keigo Takahashi, *Director, Nippon Steel Corporation*

Tosihide Takesita, *TECNOVA*

Masaru Taketomi, *Director, Industrial Bank of Japan*

Tsutomu Toichi, *Director General for Research, Institute of Energy Economics, Japan*

Toshiaki Ushijima, *Professor, Nagoya City University; former Advisor to President, Mitsubishi Oil Company*

Masao Wakazono, *Managing Director, Sakharin Oil Storage Company*

Kenji Yamaji, *Professor, University of Tokyo*

Tadashi Yamamoto, *Japanese Director, Trilateral Commission*

Table of Contents

List of Figures, Maps, and Tables

INTRODUCTION:
THE THREE FACES OF ENERGY SECURITY

Regaining energy security became a high priority task for policymakers in Trilateral countries when the first oil shock hit in the fall of 1973. The Arab oil embargo and tripling of oil prices brought profound economic disruption felt for years to follow. The political disruption was also substantial. The Organization of Petroleum Exporting Countries (OPEC), especially its Arab component, emerged as a powerful player on the international political scene. The second oil shock at the end of the decade—and the associated Iranian Revolution—reinforced energy security concerns.

A policymaker casually surveying the international scene in the mid-1990s would conclude that energy security has been successfully regained. The threat of disruption to energy supplies is of little immediate concern. OPEC is currently weak. Since the spike in prices during the Gulf War, international oil prices, as Figure 1

FIGURE 1
International Oil Prices

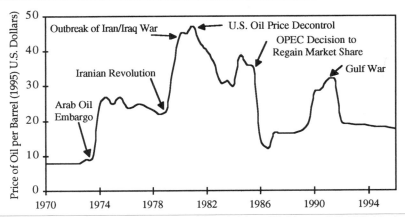

Source: *Energy Security: A Report to the President of the United States* (Washington, D.C.: DOE, March 1987); and the GEMS Global Energy Supply and Demand Model. The GEMS Model, developed by Washington Policy and Analysis, is described in Appendix C.

demonstrates, have been relatively steady at levels below (in real terms) those of the mid-1970s.

But some underlying trends arouse concern that our countries may drift into danger over time. That concern, given energy's broad economic and political importance, led the leadership of the Trilateral Commission to ask us to prepare this report.[1]

In particular, Figure 2 indicates that dependence on the Persian (or Arabian) Gulf oil exporters is rising and projects that the percentage of world oil production provided by Gulf exporters will, by 2010, edge back to the levels of the early 1970s. In energy planning terms, 2010 is not far away.

FIGURE 2
World Dependence on Persian Gulf Oil

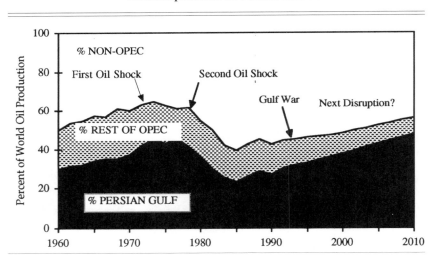

Moreover, in 2010 the Trilateral countries will constitute a significantly smaller share of much greater world energy consumption than was the case in the early 1970s (see Figure 3). The Trilateral countries need to think of energy security in a global context.

This rising vulnerability to disruption, in a more fully globalized context, is the organizing concern driving the first three, rather brief chapters of this report.

---

[1]The Trilateral Commission held its first meeting in October 1973. The oil shocks and related concerns were of major importance in shaping the agendas during the Commission's early years. The current report is, however, its first broad examination of energy issues since the 1978 report entitled *Energy: Managing the Transition*, prepared by John Sawhill, Hanns Maull, and Keichi Oshima.

FIGURE 3
Energy Consumption by Region

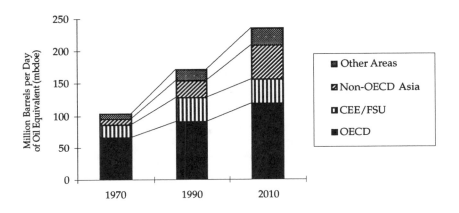

Source: GEMS Global Energy Supply and Demand Model

- Chapter I looks in more detail at the projected rise in dependence on the Gulf oil exporters. It is possible to imagine scenarios in which such high levels of dependence will not reemerge, and there are factors—policymakers can build on some of them—which may make such high levels of dependence somewhat easier to manage than they were in the early 1970s. Nevertheless, the reemergence of such substantial dependence needs to be a serious, ongoing concern for policymakers in Trilateral countries.

- Chapters II and III examine two broad areas in which Trilateral policymakers must continue to work together to limit vulnerability to disruption. Chapter II focuses on the arrangements for coordinated responses to emergencies developed in the framework of the International Energy Agency (IEA) and casts them forward in time. Some voices in our countries doubt the continued utility of strategic petroleum reserves held by some Trilateral countries and devalue IEA-centered arrangements for coordinated responses to emergencies, for sharing in solidarity the pain of disruptions. We disagree. Chapter III focuses on security in the Gulf region. The broad political/military context in the Middle East is different today than it was in the early 1970s (the 1973 Arab-Israeli War helped trigger the first oil shock), but the region remains unstable. The rise in dependence on the Gulf exporters will reinforce the importance of security in the Gulf region.

Energy security has three faces. The first involves limiting vulnerability to disruption given rising dependence on imported oil from an unstable Middle East. The second, broader face is, over time, the provision of adequate supply for rising demand at reasonable prices—in effect, the reasonably smooth functioning over time of the international energy system. The third face of energy security is the energy-related environmental challenge. The international energy system needs to operate within the constraints of "sustainable development"—constraints which, however uncertain and long-term, have gained considerable salience in the energy policy debates in our countries.

- The second face of energy security is the primary concern shaping Chapters IV-VI of this report. Chapter IV focuses on the energy policies of Trilateral countries. Chapter V focuses on energy investment and the broader energy outlook in Russia, Central Asia and the Caucasus. Russia and the Newly Independent States formed out of the old Soviet empire in Central Asia and the Caucasus constitute an area from which large additional supplies of oil and natural gas may flow on to international markets in the coming years—and the energy sector will be of crucial importance in the development of these countries. The most striking increases in energy consumption in the coming years are likely to occur in developing countries, led by China and other rapidly industrializing economies in Asia. Chapter VI focuses on the energy dynamics of rapidly industrializing countries.

- Chapter VII, our nuclear energy chapter, bridges the second and third faces of energy security. Nuclear energy technology first emerged as a means to meet rising energy demand at a reasonable cost with a supply more secure than oil imported from the Middle East; but it may be that nuclear power will make its greatest contribution to energy security in a long-term sustainable development context. If the growth of greenhouse gas emissions eventually needs to be severely constrained, the role of nuclear power may dramatically increase.

- Chapter VIII is devoted to the environmental challenge. We look first at the threat of global climate change associated with rising greenhouse gas emissions from burning fossils fuels, and then at the acid deposition and urban air pollution challenges also associated with the burning of fossil fuels.

For a decade or more, the trend has been toward greater market-orientation in the energy policies of Trilateral countries. The gains from more market-oriented policies constitute a theme that runs through many chapters of this report. At the same time, as discussions among the three of us have indicated, questions remain about how much markets can achieve. Each of the three faces of energy security provides a perspective from which doubts can be expressed. How can markets on their own take care of our societies' vulnerability to disruptions in an emergency due to heavy dependence on imported oil from an unstable Middle East? How can markets, notoriously short-term on their own, reliably take care of our societies' long-term interest in adequate energy supplies for rising demand at reasonable prices? How can short-term markets take care of the long-term challenge of "sustainable development"?

This debate becomes rather sterile if cast in either-or terms. The question for policymakers is to set the right framework conditions for markets, to utilize the virtues of markets for public as well as private purposes, to incorporate the "externalities" (protection against disruption, long-term supply concerns, environmental protection) in as market-oriented a setting as possible.

I. PERSIAN GULF EXPORTERS AND INTERNATIONAL MARKETS

The starting point for this project is the mainstream projection that dependence on Persian Gulf oil exporters will climb back to almost half of world oil supplies by 2010—levels last seen in the 1970s when they helped set the stage for the oil shocks of that decade. Some observers are skeptical that such levels of dependence will re-emerge, and the first part of this chapter addresses that skepticism. It is possible to imagine scenarios in which such levels of dependence will not re-emerge, but policymakers cannot count on them.

Some observers argue that even if dependence on Persian Gulf exporters does climb back to almost half of world oil supplies, other factors will make this dependence less dangerous. The world economy is a little less dependent on oil. Oil markets have become much more traditional commodity markets. An "integration of interests" has taken place between the Gulf exporters and international markets. The latter parts of this chapter take up these arguments one by one. Each has some merit, and policymakers can build on them to some extent, particularly in encouraging a deeper integration of interests. But these arguments are not strong enough to obviate the need for Trilateral countries—as discussed in Chapters II and III—to keep in working order arrangements for coordinated responses to emergencies and to give active attention to security in the Gulf region.

A. PERSIAN GULF EXPORTERS AND WORLD OIL SUPPLIES

First we must address the skepticism—expressed by a number of those with whom we consulted—that dependence on the Persian Gulf exporters, which declined by about half (as a percentage of world supplies) from the mid-1970s to the mid-1980s, will climb back to mid-1970s levels by 2010.[1] At the heart of this uncertainty are the

---

[1] The six principal Persian Gulf oil-producing countries are Iran, Iraq, Kuwait, Qatar, Saudi Arabia, and the United Arab Emirates. Approximately two-thirds of the world's proved recoverable oil reserves are located in the Persian Gulf region.

remarkable increases over the intervening years in actual and forecasted non-OPEC oil production.[2]

Both new technology and more stable fiscal regimes are large parts of this story. Advancements in the drilling and testing process, combined with innovative three-dimensional (3-D) seismic technology, have led to improved accuracy and a reduction in exploration drilling costs. Three-dimensional seismic surveys, which became widely used in the 1990s, have dramatically improved exploration capabilities. Development costs have been reduced by horizontal drilling, which has two main advantages. First, it reduces the necessity to relocate the rig. Second, it limits the area of contact with the oil-bearing rock as the rig drills at a shallow angle. The story of North Sea oil illustrates the importance of these technological improvements. Norway is now the second largest crude oil exporter in the world and can produce North Sea oil from substantial depths at a cost of only $6-8 per barrel—a substantial reduction in cost.

FIGURE 4
Non-OPEC Oil Production Forecast

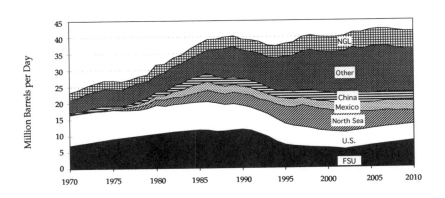

Source: Exxon Corporation

Non-OPEC oil production has also benefited from greater access to underdeveloped areas of the world. Figure 4 indicates the increased importance of "other" areas in non-OPEC oil production over time.

---

[2]Approximately three-quarters of total worldwide oil and gas investment is being spent in high-cost OECD countries, yet the OECD region as whole has only 6 percent of proven reserves of oil, and it is doubtful this share will ever increase.

There now are approximately 80 oil-producing countries in the world.

We recognize the remarkable increases in actual and forecast non-OPEC oil production. These increases are incorporated in our own projections. But, to assume a further major expansion of non-OPEC oil production is more than current analysis permits. The increases in forecasted non-OPEC production have done little more than turn a forecasted decline into relatively steady production out to 2010 at somewhat over 40 million barrels per day.

With projected increases in worldwide oil consumption (see Figure 5), steady non-OPEC oil production represents a declining share of total world oil supplies. The IEA estimates that world oil demand will rise from the 1994 level of 68 million barrels of oil per day up to between 90 and 97 million barrels per day in 2010.

FIGURE 5
World Oil Demand

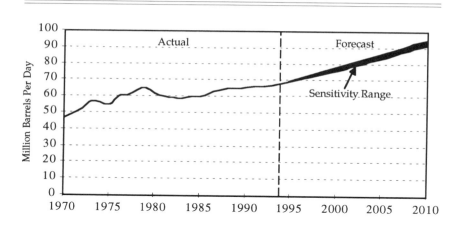

Source: International Energy Agency

Energy efficiency gains are an important factor in the path of demand growth. Energy efficiency has improved 1-3 percent per annum in IEA countries, where there is potential for further improvement. The potential is yet greater in developing countries and the countries in the area of the former Soviet Union and Eastern Europe, where energy consumption per unit of GDP is much higher. Identifying the potential for greater energy efficiency is not the same as its realization, however, because these gains require active implementation, including investments and consumer acceptance. The potential for further energy efficiency gains varies among sectors, with the greatest gains in the industrial sector so far. The IEA demand forecast presented here already incorporates some measure of energy efficiency gains.

Thus, despite the positive prospects for steady (instead of declining) non-OPEC supply of oil and some continuing energy efficiency gains, the world's incremental oil demand will have to be met by OPEC producers—and within OPEC by the Persian Gulf producers: Iran, Iraq, Kuwait, Qatar, Saudi Arabia and the United Arab Emirates. It is the percentage of world oil supplies provided by the Persian Gulf producers (not OPEC overall) which we project rising to mid-1970s levels around 2010. Persian Gulf exporters, with enormous reserves[3] and low production costs, promise to be the key swing producers in meeting the world's increased oil demand.

Of course there are a number of factors which could alter the projected dependence on the Persian Gulf exporters in 2010. We have already noted changes in forecasted non-OPEC production, which could change again. The largest projected increases in non-Trilateral consumption are in China, whose future course is particularly uncertain (see Chapter VI). There are great uncertainties of supply in Russia and the Newly Independent States in Central Asia and the Caucasus (see Chapter V).

Considerably higher energy prices for an extended period could call forth additional non-Gulf supplies and reduce the growth of demand. In the discussion of this report, some persons asked us to predict oil prices to 2010, from which supply and demand would follow. But this is not the way energy companies plan their long-term investments or international agencies make their projections. They look at various factors in the development of supply and demand (including factors as broad as rates of population growth and economic growth), and at the various scenarios that seem to flow from supply and demand developments. They (and we) assume that oil prices will fluctuate to some extent, and that politically motivated disruptions may bring abrupt price rises for a time. Without such disruptions, the supply and demand outlook to 2010 so far includes no dramatic, extended rise in real oil prices.

---

[3]The optimism about non-OPEC supplies is sometimes phrased in terms of the remarkable increases in proved reserves of oil in the world, even while consumption continues apace. Between 1970 and 1995 the world's proved oil resources have increased from 530 billion barrels to about 1 trillion barrels, despite the world having consumed about 500 billion barrels over that same period. However, about two-thirds of those 1 trillion barrels are in the Persian Gulf region.

In sum, it is possible that dependence on the Persian Gulf exporters will not rise to projected levels, but any reasonable plan to maintain energy security over time cannot at this juncture assume such dependence will not re-emerge.

B. THE WORLD ECONOMY'S DEPENDENCE ON OIL

Dependence on the Persian Gulf exporters for about half of world oil supplies in 2010 will be less precarious if the world economy's dependence on oil is substantially less than in the early 1970s. This will be the case for some countries, most notably Japan. When the Arab oil embargo was imposed in 1973, imported oil (Japan is without significant domestic oil production) accounted for 77 percent of Japan's total primary energy supply. Today, the figure stands at 58 percent. The 1994 Long-Term Energy Plan published by the Japanese Ministry of International Trade and Industry (MITI) projects that Japan's dependence on imported oil will continue to decline, reaching 52 percent in 2000 and 47 percent in 2010.[4]

For the world economy as a whole, however, oil will still be the single most important primary energy source in 2010. In the early 1970s, oil accounted for one-half of total primary energy demand; by 1994, this had fallen to about 40 percent. The share of oil in the world's energy mix is expected to remain relatively stable at this level over the next 15 years (the oil share in the transportation sector will continue to be much higher).

Trilateral countries pay close attention to their physical dependence on oil imports. Yet if the principal security concern is not global physical shortage, but political disruption causing economic distortion, the protection afforded by declining oil imports for one country or group of countries should not be over-estimated.

In theory, another energy source could also involve supply security complications. In the early 1980s, for example, the United States worried about Western Europe becoming too dependent on natural gas from the Soviet Union. Later in this report, we give some attention to the complicated issues concerning both gas and oil pipelines from former Soviet Republics in Central Asia and the Caucasus. There are also concerns about sea-borne transport of liquefied natural gas (LNG), of which Japan is the largest consumer.

---

[4]Ministry of International Trade and Industry, *Japan's Long-Term Energy Plan* (Tokyo: Ministry of International Trade and Industry, 1994).

Rapid growth is projected in both international pipeline and LNG gas supplies. Yet, the share of gas in worldwide energy consumption is only about three-fifths the share of oil (now and through 2010 in standard projections), and reserves and low-cost production are not as concentrated as oil reserves and low-cost oil production are in the Gulf. The many particular security issues associated with gas do not add up to the potential for worldwide economic disruption associated with the oil shocks of the 1970s, although there could be significant discontinuities on particular multinational pipeline routes due to political blackmail, sabotage, and terrorism.

C. MORE PRODUCERS, IN A TRADITIONAL COMMODITY MARKET

Oil markets are much less concentrated now than in the early 1970s, in at least two ways. First, as noted in passing above, there are many more producers. Some individuals with whom we consulted argued that this "greater diversity" of suppliers ensures and will continue to ensure that the oil market is more stable. This argument has some merit, but should not be carried too far. As we have noted in this chapter, it does not appear that the proliferation of producers will stem a rising dependence on the Persian Gulf exporters. Further, the presence of many more producers does not necessarily provide additional surge capacity that could be utilized in an emergency.

The second change—related to the first—is that oil markets have come to resemble traditional commodity markets, with many more players (including financial institutions) and the development of a futures market. The earlier system of official prices fixed by a few key exporters, or through the framework of OPEC, has disappeared—as, to a considerable extent, have administered prices in the energy markets of Trilateral countries (see Chapter IV). There are strengths from an energy security perspective in this shift to traditional commodity markets for oil and other energy products. Such markets are more transparent. They respond more quickly and flexibly to changing circumstances. On the other hand, the energy security virtues of these markets should not be oversold. Without the right framework conditions set by public authorities and the coordinated management of emergency stocks, speculative purchases (as in the second oil shock in 1979) can exaggerate price movements and the economic disruptions associated with them. And very large suppliers can still exercise substantial power in tight markets.

D. THE INTEGRATION OF INTERESTS

In the early 1970s, the Gulf exporters and their OPEC colleagues were in many cases operating recently nationalized production operations. The confrontations which accompanied the nationalization process made more natural the confrontations embodied in the oil shocks of the 1970s. The major exporting countries saw themselves standing apart from the Organisation for Economic Co-operation and Development (OECD) "consuming" countries, and raised the banner of a New International Economic Order, a cause in which they sought to enlist the non-oil developing countries as well.

Over time this context has changed. During the 1980s and 1990s there has been steady integration between upstream and downstream activities. The cooperation between the German oil company VEBA and Venezuela is a good example, as is the case with Saudi Arabia and the Texaco network. Producer countries have purchased refineries in the United States and Europe and expressed an interest in downstream purchases in Japan. Such downstream investments allow producers to capture some of the profits from refined products; and at the same time give them a larger stake in the economies of the consuming countries. Broader investments in the economies of the consuming countries also serve an integrating purpose. Policymakers can build on this integration of interests, but it does not solve the problem of potential disruptions.

II. COORDINATED RESPONSES TO EMERGENCY SITUATIONS

Major supply disruptions in international energy markets put national governments and energy companies under maximum pressure to assure their own supplies, with little regard for others; yet these are moments when the most is to be gained from working together, from conceiving and pursuing energy security in a collective framework. Trilateral governments have learned important lessons about emergencies and how to respond to them in the years since the first oil shock of 1973-74. Part of maintaining energy security in the coming years will be to make certain these lessons continue to find expression, in collective institutions and in the thinking of policymakers, and continue to be refined to fit changing circumstances. However serene the current moment, we cannot assume that future major disruptions will not occur. Indeed, the active embodiment of these lessons in collective institutions and the minds of policymakers is an important part of deterring future emergencies, as well as containing the damage from those which do occur.

This chapter sketches the evolution of emergency arrangements among Trilateral countries since the 1973-74 oil shock and looks to the future. Two themes should be highlighted at the outset.

First is the acquired understanding that the main problem in an emergency is likely to be abrupt physical disruption of supply causing economic distortions, especially given energy's critical role in the wider economy, rather than a profound, extended physical shortage of supplies, particularly for wealthy Trilateral countries which can outbid the rest of the world for available supplies. The shortfall in world oil supplies during the 1973-74 oil embargo reached about 9 percent, but the economic and political disruption which followed was enormous, including the worst recession in the Trilateral economies in decades.[1] The

---

[1]In the United States, gross domestic product fell by 6 percent between 1973 and 1975, while unemployment doubled to 9 percent. In Japan, gross domestic product declined in 1974 for the first time since the end of World War II. The economic impact on Europe was correspondingly severe. The first oil shock came on top of delayed structural adjustment in many Trilateral countries. Fear of ongoing physical shortages compounded the disruption. A number of Trilateral countries tried to insulate their national economies from disruptions to the world economy, but without much success. The impact on oil-importing developing countries was even worse. The rise in oil prices created unmanageable demands for hard currency to finance increased balance of payments deficits.

shortfall in 1979 reached only about 5 percent of world supplies, but again brought substantial economic and political disruption in its wake, not only for Trilateral countries, but also for heavily indebted non-oil developing countries.

These collective insights—that the main problem is likely to be economic and political disruption rather than extended physical shortage, and that disruption should be approached from an international perspective—have been critical in the development of more sophisticated, more market-oriented, coordinated responses to emergency situations. This new understanding has also been crucial to the Trilateral countries' push for more market-oriented policies in the energy sector more generally (see Chapter IV below).

The second theme which runs throughout this chapter is the importance of the IEA, created after the first oil shock. Today, the IEA remains a vehicle for collective thinking and action and for sharing in solidarity the economic hardship which stems from energy market disruptions.

A. THE FIRST OIL SHOCK

Responding to the first oil shock, U.S. Secretary of State Henry Kissinger convened members of the OECD for a conference in Washington, D.C., to discuss coordinated responses to energy emergencies. The Washington Energy Conference led to the establishment of the International Energy Program (IEP) in November 1974, the founding charter of the International Energy Agency (IEA). Consuming countries aimed to avoid another oil shock and decrease their vulnerability. In addition to the commitment that participating countries hold stocks equivalent to ninety days of net oil imports, the IEP defined an integrated set of emergency response measures—stock draw, demand restraint, fuel switching, surge oil production, and sharing of available supplies—for international disruptions involving a loss of 7 percent or more of oil supply to the group as a whole or any individual country. The IEA would be charged with managing the IEP (and, more broadly, with improving the energy policies of its member countries).[2] Henry Kissinger described

---

[2]For major oil disruptions that do not reach the 7 percent target threshold (the "trigger") defined in the IEP, the IEA has a complementary set of measures known as the Co-ordinated Emergency Response Measures (CERM). These provide a rapid and flexible system of response to actual or imminent oil supply disruptions. They may also be used on the decision of the IEA Governing Board in a trigger situation. In addition to the emergency response system, the IEA countries agreed on Long-Term Programmes for the energy sector by supporting energy efficiency, diversifying resources and developing new energy technologies. In 1993 the objectives were adjusted to the changed circumstances, with an emphasis on making energy economies more flexible and able to respond to the changing global economy. These objectives are outlined in the IEA's *Shared Goals* (please refer to Appendix B).

the underlying premise in a February 1974 speech just before the Washington Energy Conference opened:

> (W)e thought it essential that those nations that consume and import 85 percent of the world's energy meet first, because they have a common problem of a very large size, that is manageable by cooperative effort only; and that will surely lead to the ruin of everybody if it is attempted to be settled on a unilateral basis.... (I)f every nation adopts a policy of beggaring its neighbors a collapse of the world economy will be inevitable and the whole structure of cooperative world relationships that has developed since the war will be in jeopardy.[3]

B. THE SECOND OIL SHOCK AND THE BEGINNING OF THE IRAN-IRAQ WAR

The Trilateral countries failed the test, however, during the late 1970s when the Iranian Revolution resulted in a rapid loss of about 4.5 million barrels of oil per day from the market. The amount was not sufficient to activate the 7 percent trigger in the IEP. Instead of drawing down stocks and sharing limited supplies, concern about an ongoing physical shortage of oil resulted in unusually heavy oil-stock building, which drove another leap in oil prices. The governments of IEA countries spent inordinate amounts of time arguing about individual country oil import goals to constrain demand, with little immediate relevance and little idea how they would be implemented. Meanwhile, the world economy was thrown into another deep recession.

The Iran-Iraq War began at the end of September 1980. Once again the world was confronted with a serious disruption in oil supplies. Meeting within days of the commencement of the Iran-Iraq War, the IEA Governing Board, chaired by Hiromichi Miyazaki of Japan, agreed to restrain abnormal purchases on the spot market and to coordinate the draw-down of stocks. Recognizing that stock build-up had resulted in exaggerated price increases, IEA countries agreed on October 1, 1981 to lower stocks. The one-page communiqué represented a major shift in IEA thinking, moving away from demand restraint and oil import targets toward stock release—which was easily calculable by traders, producer countries,

---

[3]Henry Kissinger, *Years of Upheaval* (Boston: Little, Brown and Company, 1982), p. 906.

and others interested in driving up the price. These IEA actions proved far more effective than previous efforts to contain the price during an emergency.

C. THE "TANKER WAR" AND THE GULF WAR

As the Iran-Iraq War spread into the Persian Gulf during 1984 and 1985—the so-called tanker war—there was an effort to coordinate political-military efforts with economic and energy realities. A U.S.-led effort to increase the defensive military capability of the neighboring Arab states was coordinated with an IEA-wide effort to build strategic oil stocks and to develop means for coordination in times of emergency. While stock draw policies were never actually activated and the Iran-Iraq War ceased a few years later, these activities in 1985 and 1986 provided the foundation for a successful defense of Kuwait and Saudi Arabia during the Persian Gulf War 5 years later—demonstrating that energy security requires foresight and years of preparation.

The fighting of the Gulf War in 1990 and 1991 and the handling of the associated oil market disruption drew on almost 20 years of experience of struggling to cope with such emergencies. Military preparations were in place to move a half million soldiers to the Persian Gulf region; and the IEA was primed with alternative tools to mitigate the impact of an oil disruption, including the original IEP 7 percent trigger, strategic stocks, demand restraint strategies, and opportunities to tap surplus productive capacity, especially in Saudi Arabia. The Executive Director of the IEA, in consultation with member governments, was well-informed about oil markets and, through contact with coalition governments, was able to effectively coordinate oil and energy strategies with military and political developments—and for the first time offered stocks to the world market. The price of oil rose sharply to $30 per barrel but decreased soon after order was restored in the Persian Gulf. IEA countries acted together at this time of crisis and demonstrated their resolve to play their part in the geopolitical strategy.

D. LOOKING TO THE FUTURE

If a major oil market disruption were to occur 5 or 10 years from now, would the Trilateral countries be prepared? One concern is stocks in Trilateral countries. There is talk in the U.S. Congress about selling part of the 600 million barrels of oil in the U.S. strategic petroleum reserve. Other IEA governments are not building stocks. Spare capacity throughout the world has been reduced and oil companies, for reasons of economic efficiency, are holding smaller inventories for their transportation and distribution systems.

Second, as we look to the future, oil demand is increasing rapidly in non-IEA countries. Trilateral countries should urge the rapidly industrializing countries of East and South Asia to build strategic stocks. The IEA should make a special effort to encourage their participation in selected IEA activities devoted to emergency and oil market matters. Lines of communication should be established and used. These countries' expanding share of world oil consumption will make it increasingly important to include them in emergency sharing strategies.[4]

Third, the IEA must remain a viable institution for consultation, both formal and informal. Aside from emergency arrangements, the IEA's value also lies in its coordinating function for a wide range of energy and environmental activities which serve member governments. It also has served as a useful mechanism for reaching out to non-member governments, including Russia and China. Efforts to reduce the IEA budget should be minimized and its core of some seventy-five professionals should be maintained.

Fourth—and anticipating the next chapter—the United States, consulting and coordinating with other countries, should continue to protect the Gulf region from possible aggressors. All IEA countries have a special interest in avoiding the development of weapons of mass destruction in the region and should work toward that objective bilaterally and through multinational frameworks.

---

[4]OECD countries will account for approximately half of total world oil consumption in 2010, a drop from 60 percent in 1995. Between 1992 and 2010, OECD countries will account for only about a quarter of the expected annual increase in oil demand. The dynamic economies of East Asia and China will account for a greater increase in annual oil demand than the whole of the OECD.

III. Security in the Persian Gulf

Economic and political stability in the Persian Gulf region (see Map 1) is an essential element of maintaining energy security. Each of the oil market disruptions or potential disruptions noted in the previous chapter was linked to instability in the Gulf region. Sometimes the primary threat is *internal* in a key producing country—such as the collapse of the Shah's regime in Iran which brought on the second oil shock in the late 1970s. Sometimes the primary threat is *external* to a key producing country—such as Iraq's invasion and annexation of Kuwait in 1990 or the war between Iran and Iraq in the 1980s. Relations between *Israel and its Arab neighbors* constitute the third broad dimension of security challenges in the region linked to energy

MAP 1
The Persian Gulf Region

security. The Arab-Israeli "October War" in 1973 triggered the imposition of the Arab oil embargo and the first oil shock.

Trilateral policymakers, with the United States in the lead, have contributed to the Arab-Israeli peace process and to addressing external threats—though Trilateral countries have often found it hard to work together on these complicated issues. Helping governments in the region deal with internal threats is yet more complicated.

A. ARAB-ISRAELI PEACE PROCESS

Substantial progress has been made in relations between Israel and its Arab neighbors since the 1973 war. The Camp David Accords were an earlier landmark. The agreements between Israel and the Palestinians and between Israel and Jordan are more recent landmarks. The peace process, nevertheless, remains halting and incomplete.

Energy security is only one of several considerations for Trilateral policymakers in encouraging the Arab-Israeli peace process, but there is little doubt that progress on this front improves the general context for relations between Trilateral countries and Gulf producers.

Trilateral governments have sometimes found it hard to work together on the Arab-Israeli peace process. The United States has an inevitably special role, but not an exclusive role. It is easier to work together when the peace process is moving forward.

B. EXTERNAL THREATS

The primary external threats to key producing countries have come from Iraq and Iran in recent years. For much of the 1980s, the two countries were at war with each other. Trilateral governments worked to contain this conflict and to help make sure that neither country gained the upper hand. When the conflict spread into the "tanker war" in the mid-1980s, a naval presence in the Gulf provided by several Trilateral countries guaranteed the supply of oil to world markets.

Saddam Hussein's invasion and annexation of Kuwait in 1990 raised the specter of devastating oil price increases brought about by a major war in the region. The price of oil quickly increased from $18 to $30 per barrel, but then receded when it became clear the Saudi oil fields would be protected—and Saudi Arabia used its substantial surge capacity to largely replace Iraqi and Kuwaiti oil no longer flowing to international markets. A coalition force led by the United States liberated Kuwait.

Multilateral sanctions were imposed on Iraq, administered through the United Nations, aimed at eliminating the Iraqi government's programs for the development of weapons of mass destruction. An international protection regime was established for Kurdish areas in the north. The sanctions have taken their toll on the Iraqi economy. Some argue that a continued weakening of Iraq ultimately will harm the balance of power in the region, giving more opportunity to an unchallenged Iran. We believe the United Nations has chosen correctly to keep sanctions in place—except for limited oil sales for strictly monitored purposes—until Iraq complies with all its obligations under the United Nations Security Council Resolutions.

The threats from Iran include its support of terrorism, its plans to develop weapons of mass destruction, and its activities undertaken to undermine the Middle East peace process. American concerns about these threats have translated into a tough policy toward Iran including sanctions preventing American-based companies from doing business there. Passed by the U.S. Congress and awaiting signature by President Clinton as we write is an extension of sanctions to non-U.S. companies investing in Iran's petroleum sector. The United States feels strongly that Iran's militant, aggressive posture should be punished. Iran's military build-up threatens other Gulf states and Israel and could eventually lead to weapons of mass destruction which would make defense of the region much more difficult, if not impossible. The United States is urging Europe and Japan to join this sanctions effort now, rather than face a potentially far more militarily capable adversary in just a few years.

Other Trilateral countries argue that confrontation is not the best strategy with Iran, and have refused to join the American sanctions policy. European nations are doubtful of the effectiveness of these sanctions and pursue "critical dialogue" with Iran aiming to strengthen rather than weaken the more moderate forces. They have maintained their commercial activities. They argue that areas of common interest should be pursued, especially development of Iran's oil and gas reserves and possible pipeline routes from the Caspian Sea region through Iran. Some argue that U.S. actions only pressure Iran to expand its military and encourage eventual military confrontation. Japan has also taken a more cautious approach, not wishing to undercut the American sanctions policy, but hesitant to offend a potentially important long-term supplier of oil and gas.

This is a frustrating debate between the United States and its allies. The Europeans, Canadians, and Japanese deeply object to the extraterritorial nature of the impending U.S. sanctions. European governments point to various specific ways in which they have made clear, for instance, their condemnation of Iranian support of terrorism. The United States argues that these policies are not serious without sanctions, but the sanctions will not be effective unless they are collectively pursued (as in Iraq). The Trilateral governments need a high-level working group to develop a more broadly accepted, sustained policy. This is what shared leadership is about.

The Gulf War and ongoing concerns about Iraq and Iran have led to a considerable outside military presence in the Gulf region, including some 20,000 U.S. troops. Dealing with future external threats may not be as easy as in the past. The introduction of Iranian weapons of mass destruction, particularly nuclear weapons, would make it problematic for an American president to send 500,000 military personnel to the region again. Iran may feel compelled to toughen its own military to counter U.S. actions. It may seek better relations with Russia and China to offset U.S. policies. But if Iran genuinely desires a less confrontational approach by the United States, it should take steps to reduce its interference with the peace process and export of terrorism. Such a shift in Iranian policy would bring a more stable relationship with the United States and others. The alternative is an extended costly confrontation, political and perhaps even military. Ultimately, it may take a change of generation in the Iranian leadership to bring about more reasonable behavior. Iran's rich oil and gas deposits could make an important contribution in the next century, as reserves are depleted elsewhere in the world. Iran could provide important pipeline routes for Caspian Sea oil.

C. INTERNAL THREATS

No single event would agitate the world oil market more than a disruption of oil production in Saudi Arabia. We expect Saudi oil production to increase in the next 15 years, from approximately 8 million barrels per day to as much as 13 to 15 million barrels per day in 2010. The Saudis have both the reserve potential and the financial and political motivation to increase production. Despite concern over short-term debt, the financial community expects that needed investments will be made for additional oil production capacity to meet growing global needs over the next 15 years, as long as political stability and U.S. protection can be assured.

Most observers believe that Saudi Arabia is fairly stable, but analysis is difficult in such a relatively closed society and incidents such as the June 1996 Dhahran bombing (which killed nineteen U.S. servicemen) raise serious questions. The Dhahran bombing also highlights the painful irony that actions taken to prevent against external threats (the purpose of the foreign troop presence in Saudi Arabia) may complicate dealing with internal challenges.

The political system in Saudi Arabia, as in most of the other oil-producing countries in the Gulf, is far from the more open, liberal political systems of Trilateral countries. Political changes in some Gulf states—modernization of the clerical regime in Iran or the end of Saddam Hussein's tyranny in Iraq—may improve the energy security picture. Political change in others may complicate energy security. Viewed in a medium-term or long-term perspective, out to 2010 and beyond, significant political changes may occur around the Persian Gulf.

IV. TRILATERAL COUNTRIES: GOVERNMENTS AND MARKETS

There has been a strong tradition of government involvement in and regulation of the energy sector in Trilateral countries. Government involvement increased in the wake of the 1973-74 oil shock. A number of governments sought to insulate domestic markets (and thus consumers) from the sharp international oil price increases. On the supply side, a number of governments, assuming continued high prices, supported the development of relatively costly alternative energy resources (the Synfuels Corporation in the United States is an example). Governments of countries with plentiful energy resources tended to take measures to reserve those resources for domestic markets (such as the government-supported pipeline in Canada to take oil from Western Canada to the urban centers and industrial heartland of Ontario and Quebec). Governments of countries with meager domestic fossil fuel resources, such as Japan and some European countries, sought to develop domestic alternatives (such as nuclear power including fast breeders) and diversify sources of imports.

Over time, this trend toward increased government involvement was reversed. For a decade or more, the trend has been toward greater market orientation. Different countries have moved at different speeds from different starting points, of course, but the overall trend is unmistakable and continuing. Overall, the extent of market orientation in the energy sectors of the Trilateral countries is greater than before the first oil shock.

What explains the reversal of the post-oil-shock trend and the strength of the movement toward greater market orientation?

One powerful part of the story is that oil prices did not continue to rise from the levels to which the oil shocks of the 1970s pushed them. In fact, they declined rather sharply in the first half of the 1980s. Government projects based on the assumption of much higher energy prices became harder to sustain and in many cases collapsed. A two-part lesson was buttressed by this experience: (1) Governments cannot know the energy future with much precision, and cannot plan with precision for a future they cannot know. Markets more easily adjust to changing circumstances. (2) It is extremely costly to intervene against the market for an extended period of time.

A second part of the story is that greater market-orientation has been accompanied, so far at least, by relative stability (stability had been thought to be a strength of government-managed systems). The remarkable adaptability and creativity of operators in the market (both producers and consumers) seems to have buttressed that macro-stability, while technological and economic change proceeds at the micro level in remarkable ways. This lesson has been drawn not just from the energy sector but more generally, and is surely part of an overall shift in our countries since the 1980s toward greater reliance on markets. Monopolies and cartels have come under more and more pressure. Privatization has become an ongoing process in a number of countries. As deregulation proceeds in one country or energy-related sector, it seems to encourage deregulation more broadly. Some governments want to deregulate their electricity and gas sectors in order to strengthen the competitiveness of their economies. Likewise, some energy-consuming companies seek lower energy prices through deregulation to improve their competitiveness in the global marketplace.

As discussions among the three of us in the course of this project indicate, however, major questions remain about how much markets can achieve. Each of the three faces of energy security (set out in the introduction to this report) provides a perspective from which doubt can be expressed. How can markets on their own take care of our societies' vulnerability to disruption in an emergency due to heavy dependence on imported oil from an unstable Middle East? Will markets, notoriously short-term on their own, reliably focus on our societies' long-term interest in adequate energy supplies for rising demand at reasonable prices? How can short-term markets take care of the long-term challenge of "sustainable development"?

This debate quickly becomes sterile and ideological if cast in either-or terms. The question for policymakers is to set the right framework conditions for markets, to utilize the virtues of markets for public as well as private purposes, to incorporate the "externalities" (protection against disruption, long-term assurance of supply, environmental protection) in as market-oriented a setting as possible.

We already saw an interesting illustration of this in the chapter above on the evolution of arrangements for coordinated responses to emergencies. The initial emphasis after the first oil shock on demand and import restraint by government edict as the first line of defense gave way to a more market-oriented (and more successful) emphasis by public authorities on coordinated management of stocks and transparency of markets.[1] In this chapter, we will find other examples with regard to energy policy more generally. The same theme will return in the later chapter on the environmental challenge.

A. NORTH AMERICA

United States

The United States is the largest energy consumer and producer in the world. It has substantial energy resources—oil, natural gas, coal, nuclear and renewables. It is, nevertheless, an enormous importer of oil and a small net importer of natural gas—and a net exporter of coal. Its primary energy outlook over the next 15 years, as demonstrated in Figure 6, is dominated by fossil fuels.

FIGURE 6
Primary Energy Demand in the United States

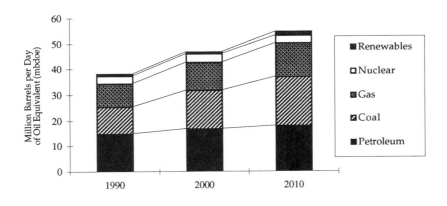

Source: GEMS Global Energy Supply and Demand Model

---

[1]How stocks should be paid for is an interesting question. One proposal in the United States (not adopted) was that the cost of building and maintaining the Strategic Petroleum Reserve—owned and operated by the government—be supported by a penny tax on each gallon of gasoline sold in the country, directly incorporating the "externality" of protection against disruption in the cost of fuel. In Germany, the IEA-related oil stocks are owned and managed by energy companies.

After a period of relatively heavy government intervention during the 1970s, energy markets in the United States are being restructured with a greater emphasis on market forces. The record to date has been positive. Consumers have benefited from lower prices. Supply constraints have eased through the opening of the North American energy market more generally.

Increasing dependence on oil imports is an issue of concern in the United States. The U.S. Department of Energy projects that by 2010, approximately 60 percent of the country's domestic oil requirements will be filled by imports. Domestic production is no longer rising, though it has not weakened as much as once predicted. Advanced recovery techniques are extending the economic lives of existing fields, and royalty relief could help the development of extensive oil reserves in the central and western part of the Gulf of Mexico. One of the largest basins of oil could lie in the Alaskan National Wildlife Refuge (ANWR). Development of ANWR should be pursued, but strong consideration should be given to restoring the environment to its natural state following development.

Natural gas markets are becoming more competitive as a result of federal legislation and regulatory reforms. The sale of natural gas at the wellhead has been deregulated, and the interstate transportation of natural gas has been opened to third parties. Environmental regulations, new gas turbines and combined cycle technology are making gas the fuel of choice for many utilities as they expand their electricity generating capacity. It is likely that at least half of all new electricity generation capacity added in the United States over the next 20 years will be natural-gas fired. Natural gas reserves in the United States, Canada, and Mexico are adequate to fuel this development.

Fifty-five percent of the electricity generated in the United States is from coal—a share that is likely to hold over the next two decades. Coal's continued viability as a domestic energy resource depends on its environmental acceptability relative to competing fuels, such as natural gas. Continued development and, more important, deployment of clean coal technologies will be critical if coal is to sustain its contribution to the country's energy mix.

Economic and environmental issues associated with plant operation and long-term waste disposal are impeding future growth of installed nuclear capacity in the United States. No new nuclear plants have been ordered since 1978, and none are expected. The Nuclear Regulatory Commission (NRC) is trying to improve the regulatory environment for the construction of a new generation of plants by expediting the licensing process and encouraging the standardization of designs. Maintaining and upgrading existing plants will be a major priority for utilities in the short-term. The Department of Energy is continuing its funding for advanced reactor designs. We think this is important. The United States will need to expand its nuclear energy capacity after 2010, given environmental and oil import concerns.

Most electricity generated from renewable energy sources comes from hydropower, which generates approximately 10 percent of the country's electricity. Other renewables, such as biomass, photovoltaics, wind, geothermal and passive solar, generate less than one percent of total electricity. Technological improvements and cost reductions have improved the economic viability of these renewables, but they are not expected to increase their share of generated electricity over the next 15 years.

The electric power sector is the largest direct energy consumer in the United States, using a third of all primary energy consumed in 1994. The industry—including investor-owned, municipal and cooperatively owned, independent, and federally-owned power—is undergoing a massive restructuring.[2] The next several years will see a transformation of the industry, affecting its organizational structure, the products and services it delivers to customers, and the federal and state institutions that regulate it. The transformation of the industry is being driven by a combination of forces, including:

- broad recognition that electricity generation no longer is a natural monopoly and could be substantially deregulated;

- statutory changes, such as the Energy Policy Act of 1992, that promote increased competition in bulk power markets;

- large disparities in electric rates among utilities, which encourage customers to seek access to lower cost suppliers;

- new low-cost generation technologies, which offer cheaper power and reduce the economic value of existing traditional generation equipment; and

- successful experience in recent years with reduced regulation in other industries (e.g., telecommunications).

---

[2]This restructuring is often termed "deregulation." Deregulation is sometimes, however, leading to more regulation at the state level. For example, in California and Massachusetts, state bodies are becoming more involved in regulation.

Although the trend toward greater competition in the electric power sector is likely to continue, there are several issues that need to be addressed before it will be fully implemented. One of the most important issues is "stranded costs." As many utilities move into a more competitive environment, substantial fixed costs approved for recovery under the traditional regulatory regime are likely to be stranded—unrecoverable at market rates. Exposure to such stranded costs will threaten the credit rating of a number of utilities in the northeast and western United States.[3] The extent to which the owners of these assets are forced to absorb the loss in economic value or are able to recover costs during a transition period will partly determine the structure of the emerging competitive industry.

Canada

Canada has a large and diversified energy resource base with major reserves of oil, natural gas, coal, hydropower and uranium. Canada is a net exporter of coal, oil, gas, and electricity—the last two entirely to the United States. The four western provinces (British Columbia, Alberta, Saskatchewan, and Manitoba) produce oil, natural gas, coal, uranium and hydropower in excess of Canada's demands. There are significant untapped oil and natural gas fields in northern Canada. Ontario and Quebec import oil, coal, and natural gas, and are also producers of nuclear power (Ontario) and hydropower (Quebec). The Atlantic provinces import most of their oil from the North Sea. There is, however, coal in Nova Scotia and New Brunswick, considerable hydro production in Labrador, and significant potential for oil and natural gas offshore. Figure 7 projects Canada's primary energy demand over the next 15 years.

The evolution of the Canadian energy sector is a prime example of how Trilateral countries shifted from increased reliance on government intervention after the first oil shock toward greater reliance on market forces. The Canadian energy sector, especially oil and natural gas, was heavily regulated between 1973 and 1985. Importers and exporters were subjected to a complicated set of compensation payments, tax and levy rebates, and export charges intended to maintain a price to Canadians lower than world market levels. Investment subsidies encouraged tar sands and new oil production.

---

[3]Moody's Investor Services estimates the possible range of stranded costs for U.S. investor-owned utility companies at $50 to $300 billion, depending on market price assumptions. Under the most likely scenario, stranded costs will total some $135 billion. This compares to current total industry equity of about $165 billion and total assets of $570 billion.

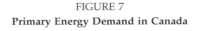

FIGURE 7
Primary Energy Demand in Canada

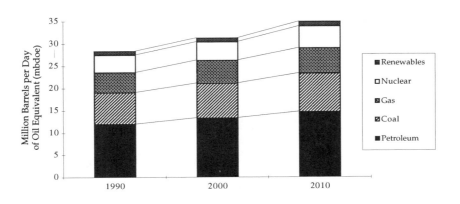

Source: GEMS Global Energy Supply and Demand Model

Since 1985, however, when the National Energy Policy (NEP) was abolished, the Canadian energy sector has experienced a fundamental restructuring, with an increasing emphasis on market forces. Oil prices were deregulated in 1985 and natural gas the following year.

In 1988, negotiations between Canada and the United States regarding the Free Trade Agreement (FTA) were completed. A key element in the negotiations was energy. Although the energy trade was largely deregulated beforehand, the FTA brought several new requirements for both countries: phase out all existing tariffs, prohibit new tariffs, minimize export price requirements and export taxes, and eliminate most restrictions on energy exports and imports. The disengagement of government from the energy sector is an ongoing process in Canada, at the federal and provincial level.

Historically, Canadian energy policy has focused on both hydrocarbon development and on attempts by the federal government to balance the interests of producing provinces as resource owners with the goal of ensuring that all Canadians enjoy the same opportunities for economic growth. Efforts to reconcile the aspirations of producing provinces—especially Canada's largest oil-producing province, Alberta—with those of consuming provinces has, over the past three decades, involved the full spectrum of intervention. Canada adopted higher-than-world prices in the 1960s, lower-than-world prices in the 1970s, and total deregulation of oil prices beginning in 1985. Deregulation and increased foreign investment have resulted in an augmentation of Canadian oil production levels, with Canada not expected to become a net importer until after 2010. The cost of extracting heavy oil from Alberta's tar sands, now producing several hundred thousand barrels of oil per day, has been reduced as a result of enhanced technology.

Production of natural gas has increased by over 30 percent since implementation of the FTA. The vast majority of this production takes place in Alberta and British Columbia. Exports to the United States account for roughly half of Canada's natural gas production, representing 10 percent of total natural gas consumption in the United States. Restructuring of natural gas markets in both Canada and the United States has had a major impact on Canadian gas production. Prior to the restructuring, Canadian and U.S. gas transmission networks were more or less independent of each other. The restructuring, largely as a result of the FTA and its successor North American Free Trade Agreement (NAFTA), has resulted in emergence of a more integrated North American natural gas market.

During the early decades of this century, coal was the dominant source of energy in Canada. By the 1960s, however, oil and gas began replacing coal for space heating and industrial use. Today, coal is used largely in the steel-making industry (metallurgical coal) and by utility companies (thermal coal) in four provinces: Alberta, Saskatchewan, Ontario and Nova Scotia. Still, it is an important export commodity for Canada, the world's fourth largest coal exporter.

Nuclear energy accounts for almost a fifth of Canada's electrical generation. There are twenty-two units in operation, twenty operated by Ontario Hydro, a provincially-owned crown corporation. The country relies on the domestically designed and built CANDU (Canadian Deuterium Uranium) reactors. For the moment, there are no plans for expansion of nuclear generating capacity in Canada. Concern over maintenance, decommissioning costs and slow growth of electricity demand are hampering any expansion plans. This bleak domestic outlook has focused the attention of Atomic Energy of Canada Limited (AECL) on selling its reactor technology in international markets, especially East Asia. Ontario Hydro may consider expanding its nuclear generating capacity around 2005 when several large coal-fired electricity generating plants are scheduled for retirement.

Restructuring of the electric supply sector is occurring, but at a much slower pace than in the United States. Traditionally, this sector has been dominated by provincially-owned utility companies (with the exception of Alberta). Elements of competition gradually are being implemented (the prospective privatization of Ontario Hydro is a major example). Over the longer term, the effects of deregulation in the United States will be felt in Canada, with the rapid emergence of a North American electricity grid.

B. EUROPEAN UNION COUNTRIES

The European Union (EU) has embarked on a unique process in history: to build a Union among countries which for more than a thousand years fought wars with each other. Although the citizens of these countries are all Europeans, they have different historical, cultural, political and economic backgrounds. While the political will to build the Union is strong, this will not be achieved overnight. Laws and regulations have to be established which are acceptable to all of the members and at the same time are adjusted to today's global marketplace.

Within the Union there is strong support to liberalize energy markets, linked to creation of a "single market" more generally and with the principal goal to liberalize the internal market for electricity and natural gas. An important if limited step forward was the June 20, 1996, agreement of EU energy ministers on the long-debated directive concerning rules for the internal electricity market. However, with each country facing a different energy situation, finding a common European approach to energy markets is a challenge. Some countries are large net producers, others are consumers. France relies on one company to oversee its electricity supply, while there are several hundred—a very large number are municipal companies—in Germany. There is no energy chapter in the Maastricht Treaty.

Several countries have taken national steps toward introducing elements of competition into the electricity supply industry. In 1990, the United Kingdom's electricity supply sector was vertically separated and privatized. Power generation was largely deregulated. Only nuclear-generated electricity remains in the public sector; and even there, beginning in 1996, the most modern nuclear plants will be privatized. Figure 8 shows the trend in average electricity prices to domestic and industrial consumers, in index form, before and after privatization. Prices in the United Kingdom fell during the mid-1980s, partly due to the fall in fossil fuel prices, and then remained broadly constant over the 3 years leading up to privatization. Following the privatization, the average domestic price initially increased, up to 1992, but has since fallen to below its 1990 level. The average industrial price fell in the first year following privatization. It then increased slightly, before falling in each of the last 2 years. Sweden, Norway (not an EU member), and Germany also intend to give more impetus to liberalization of their national electricity industries.

FIGURE 8
Trends in Real Electricity Prices in the United Kingdom
(1985-1994)

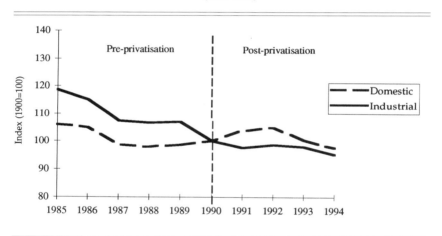

Source: UK Department of Trade and Industry

As noted above, an important first step in the EU-wide liberalization of electricity markets was taken when EU energy ministers agreed in June 1996 to a directive concerning common rules for the internal electricity market. Large consumers will be permitted to choose their supplier, including from another EU country. This first opening is too timid in the eyes of some, and there are questions about the equilibrium between individual producers. Compared to the past, however, this is progress. Further opening in the coming years is foreseen, and risks of disequilibrium should be monitored as the liberalization proceeds.

The debate over the electricity directive went on for some 6 years, with substantial disagreement among EU members. Germany, the United Kingdom and Scandinavian countries pressed for more liberalization. France emphasized preserving *le service publique* as a fundamental characteristic of its energy system, particularly for distribution and transport. The French government and Electricité de France—the world's largest electric utility—have become more open-minded about liberalizing electricity production. A compromise worked out between France and Germany led the way for the Italian Presidency to devise the June 1996 agreement.

Liberalization of natural gas markets in Europe is also proceeding. It moves at a much slower pace than in North America, in part because the industry is composed of only a few large producer and consumer companies, compared with thousands of producers and millions of consumers in the United States. In the past couple of years, proposals for introducing more competition have been intensively discussed. Those arguing for more competition are encouraged by the American experience. More competition in the United States has led to lower prices for consumers and more sales of gas by producers. Other Europeans counter that the established pattern of long-term contracts with major producers such as Norway, Algeria and Russia is necessary to develop the reserves in those countries and finance the investments in infrastructure required to bring the gas to market.

Around these government-level discussions, however, cooperation among private companies is moving ahead quickly. As elsewhere, activities of private companies, including cooperation across national borders, are pushing the political leaders down the path of restructuring. In some cases, gas companies are entering into alliances with electricity companies or with industrial co-generation companies to exploit both new business opportunities and economies of scale (e.g., joint ventures between gas distribution companies and regional electricity companies in the United Kingdom). In other cases, gas companies are looking upstream to secure direct access to gas reserves (e.g., Ruhrgas' investments in gas production in the United Kingdom sector of the North Sea).

The first EU member country in which firm governmental policy has started to be implemented in favor of more competition in the natural gas sector is the United Kingdom. In December 1993, responding to recommendations of the Monopolies and Mergers Commission, the government announced its intention to end British Gas's monopoly in the tariff market, primarily the residential/commercial market. Potential gas suppliers will be free to serve any customer, but the gas regulator will determine the limits on the volume of gas supplied to the tariff market by companies other than British Gas.

Figure 9 illustrates OECD Europe's primary energy demand outlook to 2010.

FIGURE 9
Primary Energy Demand in Europe

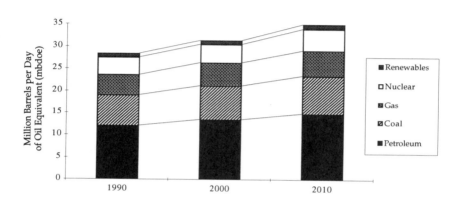

Source: GEMS Global Energy Supply and Demand Model

The common wisdom had been that North Sea oil production would peak in the mid-1990s and decline rapidly in the latter half of this decade. Improvements in drilling technology, enhanced recovery techniques, sharp cost reductions, and a stable fiscal regime, however, have changed that projection dramatically.[4] Current projections indicate that North Sea production will not peak until the turn of the century at a level over 7 million barrels per day, 1.6 million barrels per day above the 1995 level. The decline after the peak could be gentle if continuing improvements in technology and recovery techniques allow a higher recovery factor from known reserves.[5]

---

[4]This change in the North Sea oil production forecast has been at the forefront of the unexpected non-OPEC supply increase of the last several years noted in Chapter I.
[5]International Energy Agency, *North Sea Oil Supply: The Expected Peak Recedes Again* (Paris: OECD, 1995).

European coal industries have undergone a significant period of restructuring over the past several years. Overall, the size of the industry and level of production have been decreasing slowly. Coal is still an important energy resource in many countries but faces many environmental challenges. Consequently, the implementation of clean coal technologies and increasing the efficiency of coal-fired generating stations will be of primary importance.

Nuclear energy is an important generator of electricity in many EU member countries. It reduces dependence on imported energy resources and plays a key role in meeting the EU's environmental objectives. With the exception of France, however, no countries have plans to expand their existing nuclear capacity. Concerns over safety, transport and disposal of nuclear waste materials, and non-proliferation have led many countries to question the future of nuclear power. Maintaining and upgrading aging nuclear plants will be the principal activity of the European nuclear industry over the short-term. Despite the unclear future for nuclear power in Europe, we believe that EU member countries should maintain the option of renewed expansion of nuclear power in the twenty-first century.

The European Commission's 1995 White Paper sets energy policy within the general aims of the Community's economic policy: "market integration, deregulation, limiting public intervention to what is strictly necessary in order to safeguard the public interest and welfare, consumer protection, and promoting economic and social cohesion."[6] The development of European energy policy is also guided by a strong commitment to environmental quality. Promoting research and development into renewable energy technologies is a policy favored by all EU member governments. Finding a balance between the three "e's"—economic competitiveness, energy security, and environmental quality—is a central challenge confronting EU member countries.

C. JAPAN

Japan's energy consumption is the second highest among Trilateral countries (though less than one-fourth of U.S. consumption). Over 80 percent of Japan's energy needs are met by imports—including virtually all of its oil, about 70 percent of which originates in the Middle East. Consequently, diversifying its energy supply structure

---

[6]European Commission, *An Energy Policy for the European Union* (1995), p. 1.

(in an environmentally sensitive manner) is the primary objective of Japanese energy policy. Figure 10 shows Japan's primary energy demand outlook over the next 15 years.

FIGURE 10
Primary Energy Demand in Japan

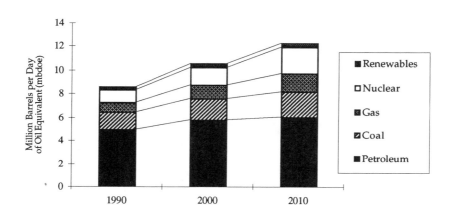

Source: GEMS Global Energy Supply and Demand Model

In 1994, Japan's MITI released its latest Long-Term Energy Plan. The plan reflects the government's determination to respond as effectively as possible to energy security requirements, to cope with increasing energy demand, to deal with global environmental problems, and to maintain economic competitiveness. The three principal objectives of MITI's Long-Term Energy Plan are to:

- maintain economic growth at an average annual rate of approximately 3.5 percent from 1994 to 2010;
- continue with diversifying energy supplies through increased use of natural gas and nuclear power; and
- stabilize CO_2 emissions on a per capita basis in 2000 and beyond at about the same level as in 1990.

When the Arab oil embargo was imposed in 1973, oil imports accounted for 77 percent of Japan's total primary energy supply. Today, the figure stands at 58 percent. This decline can be attributed to the government's policy of reducing dependence on oil imports through improved energy efficiency and active development of alternative fuels such as coal, natural gas, and nuclear energy. MITI estimates that oil dependency will be reduced further to 52 percent in 2000, and 47 percent in 2010.

Natural gas—in the form of LNG—continues to increase its role in Japan's energy mix. In 1993, Japan imported 95 percent of its LNG, or 40 million tons, of which 77 percent was imported from ASEAN countries. MITI projects that LNG imports will increase to 53 million tons in 2000 and to 58 million tons in 2010. As we have noted elsewhere, natural gas has the environmental advantage of burning more cleanly than coal or oil.

Japan is the world's largest coal importer. Its most important supplier is Australia. In 1992, Japan imported 119 million metric tons of coal, or 94 percent of its total requirements. This energy source played an important role in reducing dependence on imported oil. Coal consumption in Japanese industry increased 6 percent between 1973 and 1990, while oil consumption decreased by 29 percent. Coal consumption will increase to 130 million tons in 2000 and 134 million tons in 2010.

Nuclear energy plays a key role in diversifying Japan's energy supply, is a major contributor to the Japanese energy mix and is expected to expand its role in the years ahead. The Japanese nuclear program also benefits global energy security by decreasing demand placed on international oil and natural gas markets. Japan is promoting the establishment of a closed fuel cycle (see Chapter VII). This long-term program, which envisions commercialization of fast breeder reactor technology around 2030, aims to slow the increase in Japan's energy imports and help reduce greenhouse gas emissions. The December 1995 leakage of sodium at the prototype breeder reactor, Monju, could delay the long-term program a couple of years and result in an increase in Gulf oil imports, but Japan remains committed to the long-term program. Any slow-down in the growth of nuclear generating capacity in Japan would result in increased demand (and higher prices) for oil and natural gas on international markets.

Deregulation of Japan's petroleum industry will involve the liberalization of the domestic product market. Several amendments to Japan's Electric Utilities Industry Law will increase the competitive nature of the Japanese electric utility industry. Although the IEA review of Japan has called for accelerated efforts to deregulate and open markets, the Japanese government and industry are seeking an evolutionary—not revolutionary—path, carefully balancing free market benefits with the need for long-term reliable and secure sources of supply.

V. Energy Investment in Russia, Central Asia, and the Caucasus

The vast energy resources in the area of the old Soviet Union gave energy a central place in its economic and political life. This remains the case for Russia and even more so for some of the Newly Independent States formed out of the old Soviet empire in Central Asia and the Caucasus. The development of the energy resources of these countries in the coming years could make a significant contribution to energy security in the wider world economy.

A. OVERVIEW OF RUSSIAN ENERGY SECTOR

Energy should be an engine of growth for Russia. As shown in Figure 11, energy accounted for approximately 15 percent of Russia's gross domestic product in 1994. For this potential to be realized, however,

FIGURE 11
Russian Energy Sector and the Economy

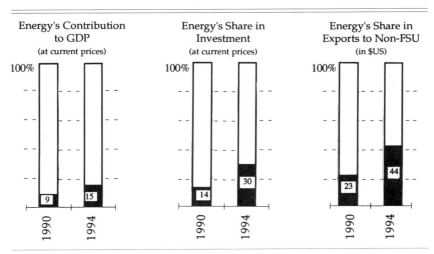

Source: Goskomstat and IEA

there needs to be continuing implementation of market-oriented reforms. This includes restructuring the domestic energy market, and expanding Russia's energy relations with the rest of the world. If properly managed, these reforms will enable Russia's vast energy resources to become a major contributor to the general welfare of the country. If poorly managed, an inefficient energy industry will delay Russia's economic and democratic transformation.

Russia currently ranks third in the world behind Saudi Arabia and the United States in oil production. However, the country's output has fallen over 40 percent since it peaked in 1987 at 12.5 million barrels per day. The precipitous decline has less to do with deficiencies in the oil reserve base and technology than with underlying political, economic, and organizational problems related to an ongoing economic transition. The large fields (particularly in western Siberia) that carried past production levels are now depleted and investment has collapsed. Production levels will likely bottom-out in 1996, and then slowly increase. The majority of this production will be consumed within the domestic market.

While there are problems in the Russian natural gas sector, it is a relatively successful industry that is able to produce an important commodity for both domestic and international consumption. Russia is the world's largest natural gas producer and exporter. The industry is dominated by Gazprom, the Russian joint stock company, which produces almost all of the country's natural gas and owns all of its high pressure transmission lines and associated infrastructure. One of the biggest challenges facing Gazprom is the age and unreliability of its gas trunkline system, including both pipelines and compressor stations. Out of 140,000 kilometers of trunk pipeline, only 7 percent was built in the past decade. The need for refurbishment will accelerate over the next decade.

Russia's gas reserves could support much higher levels of production than the current level. There are at least three uniquely large reservoirs underdeveloped in Northern Siberia. There are also arrays of large and medium-sized underdeveloped fields closer to the existing pipeline infrastructure in Siberia. As gas prices for Russian consumers continue to be increased, demand may fall, making additional export volumes available which could help pay for expanding the export pipelines toward consuming markets in Europe and eventually East Asia.[1] The

---

[1] Increasing air pollution in many of East Asia's largest cities is leading them to consider alternatively fueled vehicles, including those using compressed natural gas (CNG). Although emissions of nitrogen oxides are at least as great as those from gasoline-powered vehicles, CNG vehicles emit comparatively little carbon monoxide, reactive hydrocarbons and particulates. This transportation option may prove to be an attractive market for Russian natural gas.

rate of development of Russia's gas reserves will be determined by investment and the expansion of markets, rather than resource constraints.

Coal's role in Russia's energy mix has been on the decline since the late 1980s. The decline is the result of decreasing demand, coupled on the supply side with growing inefficiencies in the coal mining industry and lack of investment in plant and equipment. Purchasers are often unable to pay their bills, leaving the industry extremely short of cash.

Russia's nuclear energy program—which under the former regime benefited from preferential funding, better materials, better trained workers, and a stronger and broader research and development base—is facing many uncertainties. A serious financial crisis (linked to a shift in military priorities away from the nuclear industry) coupled with heightened concern over the safety of nuclear plants cloud the industry's future. Yet, the Ministry of Atomic Energy and Industry remains optimistic and has announced a program that would double installed nuclear capacity by 2010. While this goal may be unreachable, it is clear that the Russians view nuclear power as an important domestic industry, with export possibilities.

Russia has a poor record of energy efficiency. Although estimates vary, experts within and outside Russia agree that the potential for cost-effective efficiency improvements is enormous. The Institute of Energy Research of the Russian Academy of Sciences estimates the potential for energy conservation in Russia at 40 to 45 percent of current consumption. These estimates, made at current prices, are substantially higher than comparable figures for the OECD countries. The underlying reasons for the inefficient use of energy in Russia include artificially low energy prices, lack of metering and controls, a pre-eminent focus on meeting production goals, limited availability of energy efficient equipment, and a monopolistic fuel and energy supply system. The inefficiency of energy use in Russia reduces economic productivity, consumes badly needed capital, contributes to environmental problems, and employs energy resources that could otherwise be exported. More aggressive steps toward economic restructuring and energy price reform, combined with consumers paying their bills, would contribute to a more rational system. However, it will take time for the system to change. In OECD countries, with over 20 years experience with energy efficiency policies, much remains to be done.

B. FOREIGN INVESTMENT IN THE
RUSSIAN ENERGY SECTOR

Most replacement investment and capacity expansion in the Russian energy sector will be carried out by Russian enterprises and financed by internal sources. Foreign investment can be helpful in enhancing the quality and efficiency of these investments, through transfer of technology and entrepreneurial skills and managerial know-how. Abolition of the central allocation system and the structural changes achieved so far have enhanced the interest of foreign investors in Russia's energy sector. The fact that large amounts of capital have not been engaged to date can be explained by a number of factors:

- lack of a comprehensive legal and regulatory framework;
- uncertainties in property rights and confusion over rights to physical access to mineral resources;
- an uncertain taxation system that taxes revenues instead of profits;
- export controls that restrict access to international markets; and
- pricing policies that maintain a wide disparity between internal and external prices for energy resources, especially crude oil.

A step toward establishing a better framework for foreign investors and for the energy sector in general occurred in December 1994 when Russia signed the Energy Charter Treaty. The Energy Charter Treaty is a modern example of an international sector agreement, in this case between energy producers and consumers, based on complementarities and mutual benefits. The Treaty embraces countries inside and outside Europe—East and West. While a fairly large number of subjects remain open for further refinement, it already establishes within the energy sector legal rights and obligations with respect to a broad range of investment, trade and other subjects (such as the transit of energy goods, competition, and the environment) and, in most cases, provides for the enforcement of these rights and obligations. The purpose of the Treaty, as described in Article 4, is to "establish a legal framework in order to promote long-term cooperation in the energy field, based on complementarities and mutual benefits, in accordance with the objectives and principles of the European Energy Charter," a nonbinding declaration signed in December 1991. The Treaty was negotiated by the Conference on the European Energy Charter. Over fifty states came to Lisbon on December 17, 1994, for the opening of the Treaty for signature. So far, the Treaty has been signed by forty-nine states, including the European Union. The signatories include almost all the countries of Europe and all the countries in the area of the former Soviet Union, as well as Australia and Japan. The Treaty will take legal effect when thirty countries have ratified it, which is expected in 1996. (For more on the Energy Charter Treaty, see Appendix A.)

The United States and Canada are conspicuously absent from the list of signatories. While the "European" character of the initial Energy Charter seemed to exclude others and there are some legal complications for the Americans and Canadians, no better multilateral tool now exists than the Treaty to protect foreign investment in the energy sector in this broad region and the integrity of international oil and natural gas transport. We recommend that the United States and Canada sign the Treaty.

To date, the dominant vehicle for foreign direct investment in the Russian energy sector has been joint ventures. These have been limited generally to the upstream oil industry, primarily in fields already producing oil. Production by joint ventures is currently around 5 percent of total Russian crude output, though it accounts for approximately 15 percent of total crude exports. About forty foreign companies are involved in these investments, which are generally predicated on short pay-back times (often with renewed or roll-over investment). Joint ventures are most affected by current fluctuations of policy on prices, export allocations and taxes; and for most foreign partners, joint venture projects have not proven to be a very profitable undertaking. The number of joint ventures in the upstream oil sector has leveled off, and Russia's attraction to such investments may decrease as pricing and tax regimes are stabilized and Russian producing enterprises' self-financing capacity improves and they become more familiar with market-oriented technology management.

Production-sharing agreements may become more common in Russia following parliamentary approval of the production-sharing agreement (PSA) law, a blueprint for contracts between Russian and foreign oil and gas companies. The PSA law is meant to implement the executive order issued by President Yeltsin in late 1993 (No. 2285, "On Matters of Production Sharing Contracts in the Use of Underground Resources") which decreed that parliamentary approval is no longer mandatory for production-sharing deals and also instructed the Russian government to ensure that the norms of the decree are enforced. The main attraction of a production-sharing contract to foreign investors is that it eliminates many of the uncertainties about tax rates and rules. The difficulties surrounding the passage of the law demonstrate the continuing ambivalence toward foreign investment.

Equity shares in Russian oil companies and Gazprom are becoming available for purchase by foreign investors.[2] In general, the equity shares available to foreigners are small and do not involve control of strategy, budgets or operations. In the long run, as disclosure standards improve and shareholders' rights are more clearly protected, foreign portfolio investment in Russian oil companies and Gazprom is likely to grow, attracted by Russia's resource potential and the strength of a few large enterprises. Such foreign equity investment will have a spin-off benefit for Russian investors because it will provide pressure for higher standards of financial disclosure and for the resolution of credit and economic restructuring problems. Foreign portfolio investment could be an important lever in moving major Russian energy enterprises toward acting as market-oriented economic agents. Enterprises which go this route will be preferred by Russian as well as foreign capital markets.

Raising capital on international capital markets is still difficult for most Russian energy enterprises. Gazprom has raised several billion dollars in long-term loans primarily due to its ability to provide collateral in the form of future natural gas production. Some long-term loans have been provided by multilateral lending institutions. For example, a $600 million loan was awarded to a number of Russian oil production associations by the World Bank and European Bank for Reconstruction and Development for rehabilitating oil wells. Such loans have been conditional upon the implementation of, or intention to undertake, reforms conducive to foreign equity investment.

As their financial strength grows, Russian energy companies such as Gazprom and Lukoil will have opportunities to invest abroad. Such investment will benefit both Russia and these foreign countries.

C. PIPELINE POLITICS IN CENTRAL ASIA
AND THE CAUCASUS

While opportunities exist for foreign investment in the Russian energy sector, the substantial oil and gas reserves of Central Asia and the Caucasus have attracted much more attention from foreign investors. The

---

[2]In September 1995, the Atlantic Richfield Company bought by tender a packet of bonds from the Russian Lukoil company, which can be swapped at a future date for 6.3 percent of Lukoil's voting shares, or 5.3 percent of its total shares.

region's two largest oil development projects are off the coast of Azerbaijan in the Caspian Sea and in the massive Tengiz oil field in the southwestern corner of Kazakhstan (see Map 2). They are models for future development in the region. Together, the Caspian Sea reserves and the Tengiz field are estimated to be larger than the North Sea and Alaskan North Slope deposits combined. The Caspian Sea reserves and Tengiz field represent a major new source of oil for the twenty-first century.

MAP 2
Pipelines from Central Asia and the Caucasus

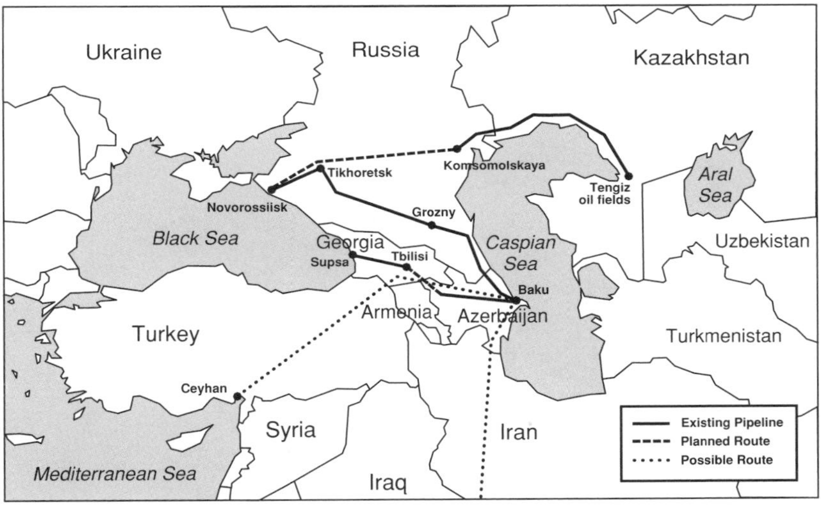

Source: "Pipe Dreams in Central Asia," *The Economist* (May 4, 1996), p.38

Transporting significant quantities of oil from this producing region to prospective markets in Europe and eventually Asia will be the greatest challenge—beyond the basic political and economic stability of the producing countries themselves. Significant investment will have to be made in transportation infrastructure, both in identifying and constructing new pipeline routes and in upgrading existing ones. Existing and prospective pipeline routes between these energy-rich countries and their future markets go through volatile areas. Transit is complicated also by a multitude of claims for hard-currency transit fees from each country through which pipelines pass. Russia, which views the region as its "near abroad," would like the exports to be transported exclusively via Russian territory.[3] Politically motivated actions by the Russians to control the flow of oil from this region are a potentially formidable obstacle.

In the days of the Soviet Union, the region relied on the Glavtransneft pipeline network. This monopoly was replaced by another body, Transneft, when the Soviet Union broke up at the end of 1991. Oil and gas from Central Asia and the Caucasus continued to be exported exclusively via the Transneft pipeline network either to the Black Sea terminal at Novorossiisk or overland to Western Europe, giving Russia considerable leverage in the region. For the region's Newly Independent States—especially Azerbaijan, Kazakhstan and Turkmenistan—development of their rich energy resources, is seen as the pathway to economic independence and prosperity. Consequently, the identification and construction of new pipeline routes which will make these countries less reliant on Russia has emerged as a top priority.

Development of the oil fields in the Caspian Sea off the coast of Azerbaijan is being carried out by a consortium of international oil companies known as the Azerbaijan International Operating Company (AIOC). The AIOC's members include Amoco, the British Petroleum/Statoil Alliance, Exxon, Pennzoil, McDermott, Unocal, Ramco, Itochu Corp. (a major Japanese trading house), Delta Nimir (Saudi Arabia), the state-owned Turkish Petroleum Company, Socar (the Azeri state oil company) and Lukoil (the state-owned Russian oil company). In September 1994, the AIOC signed an $8 billion (25-30 year) contract with the government of Azerbaijan. This production-sharing agreement calls for the phased development of the Azeri and Chirag fields and the deep-water portions of the Gunahli field. The combined estimated reserves total around four billion barrels of high-quality crude oil. Despite the enormous potential of the project, it will fail unless there is a firm and equitable agreement on transportation routes to export the oil.

Early oil, between 80,000 and 100,000 barrels per day, is expected to be produced and exported in 1997. In October 1995, the government of Azerbaijan along with the AIOC announced that two pipelines would be used to export the early oil, despite direct political pressures from Moscow on Azeri President Aliev to choose a single route that would have taken the early oil north to the Russian port of

---

[3]The division of Caspian Sea oil reserves is a question of vital interest to all the bordering countries—Azerbaijan, Iran, Russia, Turkmenistan and Kazakhstan. This issue has been under discussion since 1993. Russia and Iran assert the Caspian is a lake. Azerbaijan and Kazakhstan view it as an inland sea. If the Caspian is a lake, any offshore energy reserves—most of which lie near Kazakhstan and Azerbaijan—are, legally, the shared property of all the surrounding states.

Novorossiisk on the Black Sea. Under the dual pipeline approach for the early oil, exports will be divided equally between a route running to Novorossiisk and a pipeline from Baku to the Georgian port of Supsa, also on the Black Sea. Significant volumes of Azeri oil are likely to move through the existing Russian pipeline system before the Georgian route can be completed. Upgrading the Russian pipeline will require approximately $55 million in capital expenditures, but this is significantly less than the $155-200 million needed for developing the Georgian route. The decision to diversify the export of "early oil" is a positive development.

The AIOC is scheduled to decide in 1997 whether a larger pipeline system will be needed to handle the projected peak production of approximately 700,000 barrels per day.[4] Led by Turkey, the Western oil companies appear to be in agreement for construction of a new pipeline toward the Turkish port of Ceyhan on the Mediterranean Sea. The pipeline to Ceyhan is not favored by the Russians. They propose the development of a vast network of pipelines that would take the Azeri oil north along the Caspian's western coastline and then across southern Russia north of the Caucasus Mountains to the port of Novorossiisk. The oil would then be transferred to tankers and pass through the Turkish straits (the Bosporus and Dardanelles) en route to world markets. Turkey objects to this proposed route arguing that the resulting increase in tanker traffic through the Bosporus and Dardanelles would raise the chances of a serious tanker accident.[5]

The Tengiz oil field in Kazakhstan, with estimated reserves of 25 billion barrels of oil, is one of the ten largest oil fields in the world. A preliminary agreement between Kazakhstan and the American oil company Chevron was concluded in 1992 after 4 years of negotiation. In 1993, the official contract was signed establishing Tengizchevoil, the largest joint venture in Kazakhstan. The $20 billion deal is expected to last over 40 years. It is one of Chevron's largest investments since it began drilling in Saudi Arabia more than half a century ago.

The challenge for Chevron is not in pumping the oil out of the ground, but in getting the oil to international markets. Chevron is

---

[4]The decision to build a larger pipeline route will also be based on the status of other oil projects in the region. If these projects go well and require additional pipeline capacity to export their production, it is likely more pipelines will be built. If, on the other hand, there are no other projects of significance, the AIOC may choose to continue exporting oil through existing pipeline capacity.

[5]Russian plans have been prejudiced by the collision in the Bosporus in March 1994 between a freighter, the *Shipbroker*, and a Greek tanker, the *Nassia*, carrying Russian crude oil. The free use of this narrow channel is subject to an international convention agreed in 1936 at Montreux in Switzerland.

currently exporting about 65,000 barrels per day. This is only half of what the company hoped to be shipping by now and a fraction of the estimated 800,000 barrels per day that it hopes to export by 2010. The current exports are pumped into existing Russian pipelines. In return, Chevron gets Russian oil elsewhere that it can export to Europe.

A new pipeline will have to be constructed. The Caspian Pipeline Consortium (CPC) was established in 1992 to examine the various pipeline options for exporting oil from western Kazakhstan (particularly Tengiz) to international markets. Disputes over membership in the CPC and Russia's lack of cooperation delayed planning. In April 1996, an agreement was signed—with Boris Yeltsin and Nursultan Nazarbaev (President of Kazakhstan) presiding—for a $1.5 billion pipeline through Russia to Novorossiisk. The new pipeline will probably be built in two parts, first between Novorossiisk and Tikhoretsk. The Tengiz link would be established with the second part of the new pipeline, between Tikhoretsk and Komsomolskaya.

Natural gas is another of the region's plentiful energy resources. This is especially the case for Turkmenistan.[6] Because they cost more and take longer to construct, natural gas pipelines are a second priority. Options include a 4,000-kilometer pipeline from Turkmenistan through northern Iran to Turkey and the Mediterranean. Kazakhstan would benefit from linking into this proposed pipeline with its considerable reserves in the Uzen and Tenge fields of Mangystau. The political risk in dealing with Iran and the serious reservations of the United States government have diluted the enthusiasm for this project. Such a pipeline could eventually connect the Central Asian natural gas fields (and possibly Iranian fields) with the European natural gas grid and thereby offer an alternative to increased natural gas imports from Russia. Other options include a pipeline through Afghanistan to burgeoning markets in Pakistan and India where demand for natural gas is projected to steadily increase over the next 15 years.

The Japanese are examining the idea of building a 10,000-kilometer pipeline overland from Turkmenistan and Kazakhstan, through China and South Korea to Japan. If this ambitious scheme ever becomes a reality, the pipeline would be the longest such link in the world. It would provide plentiful amounts of natural gas to all the countries along the route. The costs of construction would be very high and

---

[6]Turkmenistan is the fourth largest producer of natural gas in the world.

probably require higher oil and gas price than today. And there are considerable political risks. Should this line or the one through Afghanistan become a reality they could provide clean and abundant natural gas to many countries, thereby reducing the need for coal burning and nuclear power in rapidly industrializing countries of East and South Asia.

The optimum solution in Central Asia and the Caucasus will be the development of multiple pipeline routes—balancing the demands of Russia, the Central Asian Republics, Azerbaijan, Turkey, and foreign oil and gas companies.[7] Special efforts should be made to involve commercially sensitive Russian energy firms, thereby giving Russia an economic and political stake in multiple pipelines. Multiple pipelines will not only enhance the security of export routes, but will also introduce greater competition and over time result in lower energy prices for consumers. If multiple transportation routes are not developed, foreign investors may begin to turn away from the region, thereby restricting its growth and preventing a major new source of oil and natural gas from coming into international markets. Pipeline routes through Iran should not be ruled out. If geopolitics were not such an important part of the pipeline questions, the preferred route in commercial terms to the growing markets in Asia would be through Iran to the Indian Ocean.

Energy can unite countries or divide them one from another. The world has enormous reserves of oil and gas, but to be commercially viable, these resources must often be transported to markets over long distances. The realities of geology and geography make it necessary that some pipelines cross through several countries from source to market. If we are to utilize efficiently the world's energy resources, we must protect against not only economic distortions, but political ones as well. Utilizing the framework of the Energy Charter Treaty and the International Energy Agency, we recommend that an intergovernmental study group be convened to discuss measures to protect the integrity of international oil and gas transport.

---

[7]The innovative provisions of the Energy Charter Treaty for uninterrupted transport should be stressed as negotiations are carried out with transit countries.

VI. Energy Dynamics of Rapidly Industralizing Countries

In the introductory chapter of this report, we emphasized that energy consumption is growing much more rapidly outside OECD countries than within the OECD group. As the Trilateral countries become a smaller portion of world energy demand, our countries need to think more than ever of energy security, as the title of this report suggests, in a global context.

A fundamental ingredient for world economic transformation in the coming decades will be meeting the energy needs of developing countries—needs woven into issues of poverty, environmental degradation, and internal political instability. Their fuels of choice will be the least expensive and more flexible ones: oil and coal. But these two fuels pose the most serious challenges for Trilateral countries—oil because of rising reliance on the Persian Gulf and coal because of its environmental impact. Trilateral countries must take a greater interest in the energy needs of the rest of the world.

The developing world[1] today accounts for more than one-quarter of global energy demand, compared with its 15 percent share in 1971. These trends are likely to continue. By 2010, IEA projections indicate that energy demand in these countries will more than double and account for approximately 40 percent of world energy demand. China and the other rapidly industrializing economies of East Asia will account for a large percentage of this increase.

Growth in developing country energy demand is related to ongoing population growth[2] (see Figure 12) as well as economic

---

[1]We follow the definition of "developing countries"—low and middle-income countries—used by the World Bank, including all the countries of Africa, Central and South America, and Asia, excluding Japan. The authors recognize, however, that some of the countries referred to as "developing countries" have per capita income and per capita energy consumption levels higher than those of some OECD countries, as well as more developed industrial sectors. The Middle East region is excluded because of the overwhelming reliance of most countries in the region on hydrocarbon fuels, both as a source of national income and as a fuel source.

[2]By 2025, the world population is projected to total 8.3 billion people, or about 45 percent more than the current estimated population of 5.7 billion. By 2050, world population projections reach 10 billion. Ninety-five percent of this increase will occur in developing countries.

FIGURE 12
World Population Growth (1750 - 2100)

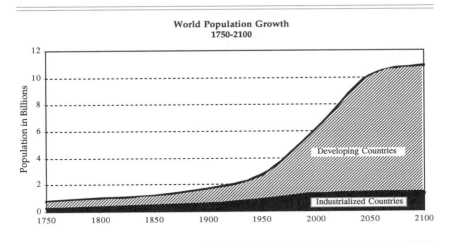

Source: World Bank

growth. Accompanying and stimulating this economic growth will be various processes, including industrialization, urbanization (the growth in the proportion of a country's population which lives in towns or cities) and the subsequent rise in demand for motorized transportation. The energy intensity (energy consumption per unit of GDP) of developing economies also tends to be much higher than in OECD economies—roughly twice as high on average at present.

The removal of barriers to trade and greater liberalization of markets have facilitated a shift of manufacturing from OECD countries to rapidly industrializing countries. Manufacturing tends to be relatively energy-intensive. Think of basic steel production shifting from the United States and Europe to Japan, then to Korea, now to Thailand and other East Asian countries, and the effects on energy use patterns. The more mature economies in the Trilateral countries are using less energy per unit of output due in part to the greater emphasis on services in our GDP. The greater energy efficiency of new power generating capacity and energy consuming equipment (including transportation vehicles) should enable rapidly developing countries to follow less energy-intensive paths than Trilateral countries did during their earlier developing phase, but this less energy-intensive path is still much higher than Trilateral countries at the current moment.[3]

We noted above the international concern surrounding increased coal-burning in developing countries and its implications for "sustainable development." Currently in China, for instance, coal represents over 75 percent of total primary energy supply and will remain China's main energy source. Aside from the global issue of greenhouse gas emissions (China is likely to surpass the United States as the largest emitter not far into the next century), there is the regional issue of acid rain (Chinese coal tends to be high-sulfur coal), with Japan and the Korean peninsula downwind. What are the alternative fuels that might slow the increase of coal-burning in China? The Chinese have set out ambitious nuclear energy objectives, some including installed capacity by 2050 roughly equal to the world's total installed capacity in 1994. With wry humor, some Japanese suggest that the prevailing westerly winds from the continent in the next century will carry either acid rain or fallout from a Chinese nuclear accident. One argument for a continued vigorous Japanese nuclear program is that it will allow Japan to participate with China and others in the region in making nuclear energy development in this area as safe as possible. We discuss nuclear energy in Chapter VII.

Four sections follow in this chapter. The first discusses prospective energy infrastructure development in rapidly industrializing countries. The second section focuses specifically on China, and the third looks at developing East Asia. A fourth section touches on other developing regions.

In earlier chapters, we noted the growing importance of the rapidly industrializing economies (as their portion of world oil demand increases) in planning for coordinated responses to oil emergencies. We applaud contacts between the IEA and China, including discussion of possible Chinese oil stocks. Increasing reliance on oil imports from the Persian Gulf is increasing energy security concerns among Chinese officials and others in developing East Asia. Trilateral countries must also be aware of another dimension to oil emergencies. The economic disruptions in the wake of the first and second oil shocks were more traumatic for non-oil developing countries than for Trilateral countries. Those leaps in oil prices were central in the developing countries' debt crisis which exploded a few years later. If the Trilateral countries take

---

[3]Exxon projects an improvement in energy/GDP ratios for non-OECD countries (outside the former Soviet Union) that would, relative to the 1970-1995 trend line, reduce energy consumption by 20 million barrels per day of oil equivalent by 2010 (more than 8% of world consumption at that time).

seriously their leadership responsibilities in the international system, this strengthens the need to keep in active working order their capacity for coordinated responses to emergencies.

A. ENERGY INFRASTRUCTURE EXPANSION

Developing countries, especially rapidly industrializing countries, will need to mobilize financial resources on an unprecedented scale for energy infrastructure projects in the coming years. The World Bank estimates the need over the next decade to be $150 billion per year. This staggering figure represents more than half of all new investment in infrastructure in developing countries.[4] One hundred billion dollars per year will be needed in the electricity supply sector, with over half of that in Asia. Figure 13 presents the World Bank's projection of the generating capacity that developing countries will need to add over the next 15 years. According to World Bank estimates, eighty percent of the money needed for energy infrastructure development will have to come from domestic savings, another 15 percent from foreign investors, and 5 percent from multilateral lending institutions.[5]

Historically, energy infrastructure development has been the preserve of the public sector in developing countries, partly on account of its perceived strategic importance and partly because the large costs and long gestation periods associated with such projects were thought to be serious disincentives to private investors. Today, several factors are pushing developing countries toward a greater reliance on the private sector.

Fiscal constraints on governments are one reason. Funding demands for health, food, welfare, and education are drawing finite government resources away from the power sector. State utilities cannot finance new investments from their own revenues because tariffs in most developing countries are not adequate even to cover existing costs. Electricity tariffs in developing countries toward the end of the 1980s were just over half of tariffs in OECD countries, and represented no more than one-third of costs.

---

[4]Infrastructure projects as a whole (power, telecommunications, piped water supply, sewerage, solid waste collection and disposal, piped gas, roads railroads, urban transport, ports, and airports) are projected to require $250 billion per year.
[5]The multilateral lending institutions include the World Bank Group (the International Bank for Reconstruction and Development, the International Development Association, the International Finance Corporation, and the Multilateral Investment Guarantee Agency), the African Development Bank, the Asian Development Bank, the Inter-American Development Bank, and the European Bank for Reconstruction and Development.

FIGURE 13
Power Sector Capacities in the OECD and Developing Countries

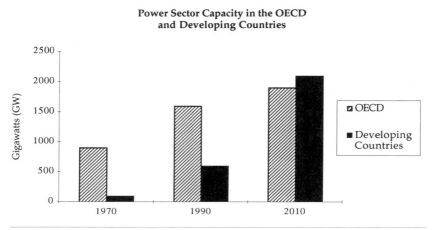

**Power Sector Capacity in the OECD
and Developing Countries**

Source: World Bank/International Finance Corporation

A growing dissatisfaction with the performance of publicly owned monopolies is another important factor promoting the shift toward greater reliance on the private sector. Lack of sufficient investment by state utilities has resulted in a backlog of unmet demand for infrastructure services in many countries, constraining economic growth.

Increasing energy demand is forcing structural change in many countries. The realization in China that it will be unable to meet projected energy demand within the existing structure is prompting the opening of the electricity supply sector to private investment.

Technological improvements have reduced the "natural monopoly" characteristics of the sector and encouraged unbundling and competition in many energy infrastructure services.[6] Independent power producers (IPPs) can build and operate relatively small plants at unit costs comparable with large generators.[7] One of the more popular IPP generating units is the combined cycle gas

---

[6]The vertically integrated, publicly-owned monopoly has been the dominant structure for the past fifty years, in both developed and developing countries. This vertically integrated structure entails the monopoly being involved in the generation, transmission, and distribution of power. With "unbundling," the three functions (generation, transmission and distribution) are separated and carried out by independent companies. For example, generation and distribution could be opened to private participation or ownership.

[7]IPPs are typically limited-liability, investor-owned enterprises that generate electricity either for bulk sale to an electric utility or for retail sale to industrial or other customers.

turbine (CCGT). A CCGT plant has many advantages: lower cost per kilowatt, shorter plant construction period, greater flexibility in terms of incremental expansion by modular construction, and higher fuel conversion efficiency.

The globalization of financial markets has multiplied financing options for infrastructure projects. The volume of transactions and the range of instruments used on international capital markets have risen.

Learning from other countries' experiences of reforming power sectors and achieving performance improvements has also proven effective. The increase in the role of the private sector has been underway in developed countries for some time. The 1978 Public Utilities Regulatory Policy Act spawned the independent power producer industry in the United States by requiring utilities to purchase power from competitive generators. The unbundling of the electricity industry in the United Kingdom in 1991 demonstrated that it is feasible to introduce competition into distribution as well as generation.

At present, IPPs are the best entry vehicle for private sector participation in electricity supply. A number of these projects are in operation or in an advanced stage of planning. Although their share of overall generating capacity is relatively small, they have facilitated the introduction of new technologies, and financing and management techniques.

Multilateral lending institutions are playing an important role in facilitating private sector involvement in power generation projects throughout the developing world. The principal role of multilateral lending institutions has traditionally been the provision of loans.[8] Today the multilateral lending institutions are becoming more concerned with assisting developing countries in establishing a framework of policies and institutions that will result in a competitive and more efficient commercial electricity supply sector.

In 1992, the World Bank adopted a series of "lending principles" designed to encourage reform in the electricity supply sector. This policy states that the World Bank will lend only where there is a demonstrated commitment to reform of the energy sector as defined by five principles: transparent regulation, market pricing, commercialization and corporatization, and demand-side management.[9] These sensible

---

[8]The power generation sector in developing countries has been a major recipient of World Bank Group resources in the past—receiving more than 15 percent of the Group's total loans.
[9]The World Bank set forth these guiding principles with the understanding that certain points would not be applicable to all countries due to differences in existing institutions and stages of development.

principles reflect the experience of the Trilateral countries and are aimed not only to attract World Bank financing, but to provide a basis for economically sound investments that will attract other financing as well.

The expansion of electricity supply through private sector involvement will require regulatory, legal, and pricing reforms that will ensure proper functioning of the market—that is, appropriate framework conditions set by governments. Each developing country will ultimately decide upon the pace and extent of its own reforms. The sheer size of the financing requirements suggests that these reforms will be critical if increasing demands for energy services are to be met.

B. ENERGY DEVELOPMENTS IN CHINA

The growth of Chinese energy consumption to 2010 and beyond is one of the biggest puzzles in the international energy outlook. Part of the uncertainty arises from the fact that we are not discussing the evolution of an established system. Tens, if not hundreds, of millions of Chinese are entering into the commercial energy system for the first time; the energy system is changing in other ways as well. Major political and economic discontinuities are not out of the question. A simple extension of the growth rates of energy consumption in recent years leads to particularly unsettling estimates, but is almost certainly too high. The GEMS model, which is the basis for Figure 14, assumes real economic growth averaging 6 percent in China over the next 15 years. Other experts estimate Chinese energy consumption in 2010 ranging from a low of about 24 million barrels per day of oil equivalent (Mbdoe) in the 1993 IEA World Energy Outlook, to about 35 Mbdoe in a 1994 contract study prepared for MITI.[10]

China is the world's largest coal producer and the sixth biggest oil producer. Until recently, China has been almost entirely self-sufficient in energy and has been able to export small volumes of crude oil and coal. However, energy production is lagging behind demand growth to such an extent that the country is now becoming dependent on imports to meet its energy needs.

In order to maintain its current level of economic growth, China will have to produce more, import more, and/or increase its energy

---

[10]We are indebted to Professor Kenji Yamaji of Tokyo University for assembling seven estimates, all made between 1993 and 1995, of Chinese primary energy requirements in 2010. We have converted his Mtoe numbers to Mbdoe.

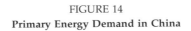

FIGURE 14
Primary Energy Demand in China

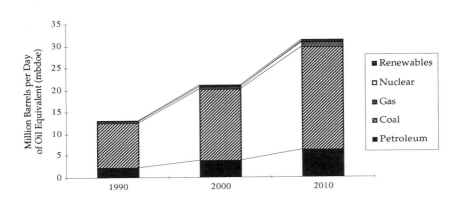

Source: GEMS Global Energy Supply and Demand Model

efficiency. There are reports that energy shortages already are a hindrance to growth. An ambitious expansion of nuclear energy is foreseen in the long-term, and there are plans for rapid growth of the natural gas industry. A major expansion of hydropower capacity is also envisioned. Yet, infrastructure inadequacies and limited capital could slow these programs.

At present, coal serves as China's principal energy resource, representing over 75 percent of total primary energy supply. Its abundance and cost-effectiveness guarantees that coal will remain China's main energy source into the next century.

There is a geographical mismatch between coal extraction and consumption. China's coal resources are concentrated in the northern and central parts of the interior, while industrially developed areas are located along the southern coast. This requires Chinese railways to transport large quantities of coal from the mines to the industrial regions. As demonstrated in Table 1, coal transport represents a significant share of the total volume of freight shipped by China's railways. Furthermore, the lack of water at the majority of China's coal mines means that most of the coal transported in China is "unwashed" and shipments contain a significant amount of debris.

Expanded coal use in China raises a number of environmental questions. Most Chinese coal has a high ash and sulfur content. The

TABLE 1
Coal Transport by Rail in China

Rail Line	Attributable to Coal Transport
Daqin Line (Datong - Qinhuandao)	100 percent
Fengshada Line (Datong - Beijing)	81 percent
Jingqin Line (Beijing - Qinhuandao)	97 percent
Shitai Line (Taiyuan - Shijiazhuang)	74 percent
Jingshen Line (Beijing - Shenyang)	59 percent
Shide Line (Shijiahung - Dezhou)	71 percent
Jingguang Line (Beijing - Guangzhou)	54 percent

Source: Japan Atomic Industrial Forum

resulting local, regional and global environmental impacts will be of increasing concern. China is already the second largest emitter of greenhouse gases in the world, after the United States, and is likely to become the largest source within the next 20 years. Acid deposition is becoming a major problem for China and is having an adverse affect on many of China's neighbors, such as Japan and the Koreas. The deployment of clean coal technologies will be of major importance if coal's adverse environmental impacts are to be addressed. The government of China has made it clear that economic growth is its top concern, not protection of the environment. The introduction of numerous environmental protection laws since the early 1980s has not slowed the pace of environmental degradation in China. International and bilateral assistance may be necessary to encourage China to utilize clean coal technologies. Significant imports of less polluting Australian coal have recently been introduced to the southeastern coastal areas.

Although China has relatively large oil reserves, and oil currently accounts for only a fifth of total primary energy supply, China became a net importer of oil in 1994. With increasing oil demand driven by the rapidly expanding transportation sector, current imports of about 600,000 barrels per day are expected to rise over time.[11] As a long-

---

[11]For an excellent overview of Asia's emerging energy situation, see Kent E. Calder, "Asia's Empty Gas Tank," *Foreign Affairs* 75:3, March/April 1996.

term solution, China is beginning to open up its Far Western Basins (Junggar, Tarim and Turpan) to bidding by foreign exploration companies. Plans to deliver the oil from the Tarim Basin to the country's populous eastern and central regions will require a pipeline that would cross 2,600 kilometers of mountains, deserts, and rivers. The financial and technical obstacles facing this project are immense. Chinese officials say construction would cost less than $1.15 billion, but some Western specialists estimate the cost at as much as $10 billion. If China is going to expand its domestic production of oil, which would mitigate its reliance on imports, foreign investors will have to be confident that a stable and transparent legal and tax framework is set in place. This is not the case to date.

Electricity generation capacity is expanding rapidly in response to surging demand. If China is to satisfy its growing demand for electricity, it will have to install one gigawatt of generating capacity per month—in other words, one large power plant per month—for many years.

The China Nuclear Corporation (CNC) has an aggressive program to install 300/350 gigawatts by 2050. This would be nine times the current Japanese installed nuclear capacity. We expect reality to fall short of these plans. China's nuclear expansion plans do indicate, however, the importance China attaches to the nuclear energy option. Natural gas, which presently supplies only 2 percent of total primary energy supply, is expected to expand its role. Its clean burning attributes make it an attractive alternative to coal.

Small-scale hydropower and traditional fuels (fuelwood, charcoal, and animal and vegetal wastes) are an important energy source in many rural areas of China. There are plans to expand China's large-scale hydropower generating capacity. The largest and most prominent example is the huge Three Gorges Dam on the Yangtze River. This controversial project, which has been under construction for a number of years, is expected to cost more than $12 billion—equivalent to 2 percent of gross national product—and to be completed by 2009.

In order to improve China's energy situation, the government has set forth a series of objectives that it hopes to implement over the next 5 to 10 years. Included in these objectives are maximizing efforts to improve energy efficiency, expanding domestic energy exploration and production, alleviating atmospheric pollution in urban areas caused by coal combustion, rationalizing energy prices, promoting technologies to raise efficiency in both production and use of energy, and expediting the construction of energy distribution systems in rural areas. Part of this energy vision is included in the government's publication, *China's Agenda for the 21st Century*, which also includes promotion of the development and use of new and renewable energy sources, specifically solar, wind, biomass, geothermal and wave. While these objectives appear sensible, there are many obstacles that will have to be overcome if they are to be achieved. The needed decentralization poses significant challenges with the structure of energy supply, demand, distribution, and pricing differing from one region to the other.

Investments in improving the efficiency of energy use may be among the wisest that China can make. Chinese and international interests overlap on this issue, and Trilateral countries should give special attention to it in technology transfer and other assistance programs.

C. ENERGY DEVELOPMENTS IN EAST ASIA

During the past decade, other East Asian countries, led by the dynamic economies of Hong Kong, Republic of Korea, Malaysia, Singapore, Taiwan, and Thailand, have experienced strong rates of economic growth.[12] Accompanying these impressive economic gains have been notable increases in energy demand. Between 1983 and 1993, total primary energy demand increased by an average annual rate of 5 percent. This was much higher than other regions of the world. Over the next 15 years, as shown in Figure 15, East Asia's primary energy demand is projected to almost double.

Limited energy resources and soaring energy demand have meant that East Asia has become increasingly reliant on imported energy sources. Approximately one-third of all the region's energy requirements were imported in 1993, including over three-quarters of its oil requirements. Increasing dependence on imports has introduced the security of energy supply—already a critical issue for Japan—as an important concern to many of the

---

[12]East Asia includes: Brunei, Hong Kong, Indonesia, Cambodia, Laos, Malaysia, Myanmar, North Korea, Papua New Guinea, Philippines, Singapore, Republic of Korea, Taiwan, Thailand and Vietnam. China and Japan are excluded.

countries of developing East Asia. Various strategies have been adopted to improve security of supply. Diversification of supply among various fuels and among various suppliers of particular fuels has been encouraged. State support for uneconomic indigenous energy production has been adopted in some countries, as has direct investment in overseas energy production.

FIGURE 15
Primary Energy Demand in East Asia

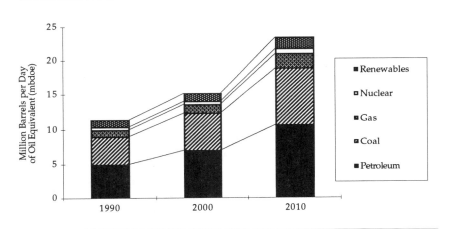

Source: GEMS Global Energy Supply and Demand Model

Energy demand growth rates will continue to be high in the medium-term (although they are likely to lower than the record rates of the 1980s). This will result in substantially increased energy requirements and energy imports. As the East Asian economies grow, the most rapid increases in energy demand will come from the residential and transport sectors.[13]

Coal has played and will continue to play a crucial role in East Asia's rapid economic development. The East Asian countries are expected to be the fastest growing market for coal into the twenty-first century. Australia will be the main beneficiary of expanded coal

[13]In volume terms, energy demand growth in the transport sector in East Asia averaged over 9 percent per year during the 1980s and surpassed 10 percent in some of the dynamic economies. In South Korea, for example, the growth in transport demand averaged almost 15 percent between 1981 and 1991.

use. By 2010, it is possible that Australia will provide over 50 percent of East Asia's coal. Indonesia also has plans to expand its coal production, both for use in its electricity supply sector and for export. Environmental concerns and the increasing competitiveness of natural gas could cut into coal's projected use.

With a few exceptions, such as in Vietnam where oil production is expected to increase over the short-term, oil production in the region will continue to fall. Falling output and rapidly increasing demand for oil (originating from the transport sector) are expected to increase imports from the Persian Gulf region. Rapid growth in oil demand in Indonesia coupled with steady or falling levels of production mean that Indonesia could become a net oil importer by the turn of the century.

Electricity demand is certain to continue growing rapidly throughout East Asia. Indonesia, Malaysia, the Republic of Korea and Thailand are among countries with double-digit electricity demand growth rates. In the past, most electricity has been supplied by integrated state-owned monopolies. The enormous financing required to build needed generation capacity is well beyond what most of the state-owned utilities can provide internally or raise from international capital markets. The result has been a dramatic increase in interest in the introduction of private capital. The resulting trend to open electricity markets to private generators is only beginning to bear fruit. The Philippines, Indonesia, and Malaysia have concluded agreements with several IPPs. The Republic of Korea and Thailand are also pursing this strategy. However, many of the other countries still lack the proper regulatory framework for full private sector participation in electricity supply. The number of East Asian power projects which will materialize is likely to be well below the level needed to satisfy all potential demand, even with a large scale move to private sector participation.

Natural gas is expected to expand its role over the period to 2010, especially in the electricity supply sector. Brunei, Indonesia, and Malaysia are the primary exporters within East Asia. The Republic of Korea and Taiwan are the largest consumers, with Thailand, China, and India on the horizon as large importers. The majority of LNG supplies originate from the Gulf countries of Oman and Qatar. The availability of pipeline natural gas will likely increase. The beginnings of a regional grid linking consumers with new gas supplies from Malaysia, Myanmar,

Vietnam, and Indonesia are being put in place. Ambitious schemes to link East Asian consumers with pipeline gas from Russia, Central Asia, China and even Australia are taking shape.

Nuclear energy is promoted strongly by governments and state utilities in several East Asian countries as a means of diversifying energy and electricity provision away from imported fossil fuels. Currently, there are only two countries with operating nuclear energy programs in East Asia—the Republic of Korea and Taiwan. The Republic of Korea plans to double its existing capacity by 2010. Additional nuclear energy programs are contemplated by Indonesia and the Philippines.

Environmental concerns continue to take a back seat to the imperatives of continued rapid economic growth in order to raise living standards. Nevertheless, the environmental effects of rapidly growing energy consumption are being increasingly recognized, and efforts to mitigate these impacts and integrate them into national economic development policies are beginning.

D. OTHER REGIONS

South Asia

The countries of South Asia are characterized by their large and rapidly growing populations and per capita incomes among the lowest in the world.[14] In both economic and energy terms, the region is dominated by India. In 1992, India accounted for more than 75 percent of the region's gross domestic product and 85 percent of the region's energy use.[15] All the region's economies have implemented some structural and macroeconomic reforms. Although varying in their extent and success, the reforms have generally led to higher economic growth rates. This expansion in economic activity has been accompanied by increases in energy demand. Over the next 15 years, energy demand is projected to increase at an annual average rate of 5 percent. The industrial and transportation sectors are expected to have the highest energy demand growth rates.

In terms of fuel structure, the region's commercial energy use remains heavily weighted toward coal, accounting for over 50 percent of total primary energy supply. Coal use is particularly high in India. In Nepal, Pakistan, and Sri Lanka, oil dominates the energy

---

[14]South Asia includes: Bangladesh, India, Nepal, Pakistan, and Sri Lanka.
[15]India's population is expected to surpass that of China in 2020.

consumption profile; in Bangladesh, natural gas is the most important fuel. Although estimates vary widely, traditional fuels continue to satisfy a substantial proportion of the region's energy demand, especially in households.

An important development in the region over the past several years, which will be a key determinant in its future energy supply structure, is the encouragement of private sector participation in energy production and supply. This has been pursued most vigorously in the electricity supply sector. The move to liberalize the power sector should, in theory, facilitate the required increase in capacity. A large number of IPP projects have been proposed, but it is uncertain how many will actually be completed. There is considerable opposition to private power provision and overseas involvement in power supply at both the national level and in some states. The framework for foreign investment remains unclear. Electricity tariffs are artificially low, and sovereign guarantees for most potential power projects are unavailable or uncertain.

Latin America

The Latin American region is benefiting from sustained economic growth,[16] spurred by widespread economic reforms, and accelerated regional integration—particularly Mexico's participation in NAFTA and the MERCOSUR customs union among Argentina, Brazil, Paraguay, and Uruguay. Energy demand has been increasing along with economic growth. Fortunately, the region has rich reserves of energy and will be relatively self-sufficient in the coming decades.

Latin America accounts for ten percent of the world's oil reserves, but reserves are unevenly distributed. Oil exploration and development has been increasing as a result of industry restructuring, privatization, and other sectoral reforms aimed at attracting private investment, both from domestic and international sources. Together, Mexico and Venezuela account for approximately 90 percent of the region's oil reserves, and more than 70 percent of crude oil production. New discoveries and development in Colombia appear promising. Venezuela's heavy oil deposits are extensive and represent an important hydrocarbon source for the next century.

---

[16]The Latin American region includes Mexico, the countries of Central and South America, and the Caribbean.

Demand for natural gas in Latin America is being driven by the electricity supply sector, where environmental advantages over other fossil fuels are a key factor. All natural gas produced in Latin America is produced and consumed within the region, except for Mexico's small imports of natural gas from the United States.

Latin America has tremendous hydropower potential because of its favorable climate and geographical conditions. Hydropower generates three-quarters of the region's electricity, including from the three largest hydropower stations in the world. The further expansion of hydropower will be dependent on availability of financing, as well as environmental concerns.

Coal plays a relatively minor role in the Latin American energy balances. Only three countries—Argentina, Brazil, and Mexico—have installed nuclear capacity. All three had major plans to further develop their respective nuclear energy programs in the 1990s, but budget constraints have forced them to reconsider their plans.

Historically, electricity in most countries has been supplied by state-owned power enterprises. Often, these enterprises were used to promote government social policy objectives and have been characterized by government involvement in day-to-day operations, poor management and accounting techniques, large government subsidies, and capital shortages. In response to these conditions, many Latin American countries have begun and are continuing major structural reforms of their electricity supply sectors. These reforms include demonopolization and privatization, and are designed to attract private investment, increase efficiency, and improve environmental performance. The changes have been most effective in Argentina, where over the past several years a large proportion of electricity supply, transmission, and distribution network assets have been transferred to the private sector. Other examples of successful reforms are in Chile, with reforms currently planned or undertaken in Bolivia, Colombia, Ecuador, Jamaica, and Peru. IPP projects are under consideration in Mexico and some Central American countries.

Africa

Africa's energy challenges are part of its broader economic challenges. Many countries have introduced restructuring programs. Subsidies on energy prices will have to be reduced if energy demand is to be met over time. Developments in South Africa could prove to be a good example for others. Northern African countries, particularly Algeria, Libya, Morocco, and Tunisia, are major energy producers and exporters. A majority of their exports are directed toward the EU. Energy relations between EU members and the North African countries are becoming increasingly important.

VII. NUCLEAR ENERGY AND LONG-TERM ENERGY SECURITY

Nuclear energy has considerable appeal from the perspective of all three faces of energy security. If the energy security problem is vulnerability to disruptions in an emergency due to heavy dependence on imported oil from an unstable Middle East, nuclear power is an alternative energy source which can reduce dependence on imported oil. If the energy security problem is the long-term provision of adequate supply for rising demand at reasonable prices, nuclear energy, at least at an earlier stage of its history, seemed to offer the prospect of abundant power at low prices. If the energy security problem is the long-term problem of sustainable development, given the global climate change implications of rising greenhouse gas emissions from the burning of fossil fuels, nuclear power emits no greenhouse gases (or sulfur dioxide or nitrous oxides that create "acid rain").

The growth of nuclear generating capacity, and planning for additional capacity, was fairly vigorous at an earlier time in the Trilateral countries. One high point was in the wake of the first oil shock in 1973-74. But in North America and in OECD Europe over the past twenty years, the push to expand nuclear power has faded. No new plants have been ordered in the United States since 1978. No new plants are in prospect in Canada. The primary exception in Europe is France, but even Electricité de France (EDF) has placed no new orders beyond the four plants now being constructed. It is a legacy of an earlier era that of the about 425 nuclear power generating plants in operation in the world, about 275 are in North America and OECD Europe (see Figure 16). Some additional plants will come on line in the years out to 2010, but the rate of increase is likely to be less than the rate of increase of electricity consumption. No additional contribution can be expected out to 2010 from nuclear power in North America and Europe as dependence rises on oil exports from the Gulf.

In Japan, although nuclear power faces in some measure the problem of public acceptance (the December 1995 accident at Monju and its handling have increased the problem), the Japanese program continues to expand. The growth of nuclear power in Japan is a vital part of its strategy to reduce dependence on imported oil from 77 percent of total primary energy requirements in 1973 to 58 percent now and, according to MITI's plans, 47 percent in 2010. Furthermore, nuclear power is a key component of Japan's environmental strategy which seeks to limit emissions from the burning of fossil fuels. With Japan one of the largest energy consumers in the world, the reduced emissions associated with its growing use of nuclear power will also benefit the global environment.

FIGURE 16
Countries with the Largest Nuclear Generating Capacity (1994)

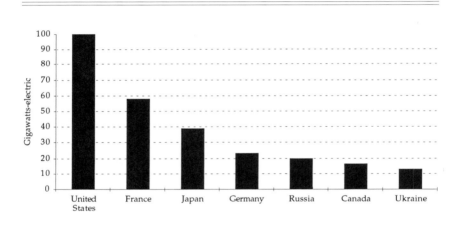

Source: Nuclear Energy Agency, OECD

Aside from Japan, the most ambitious plans for expansion of nuclear power in the coming years are in China, South Korea, and the rest of developing East Asia. Not surprisingly, these ambitious nuclear power plans go along with projections of rapid economic growth for this part of the world and a growing dependence on oil imports from the Middle East—classic energy security concerns.

In the sections that follow, we devote considerable attention to nuclear power in the United States, Canada, and OECD Europe—not because of the additional contribution it will make to energy security out to 2010, but because we hope its role can be enlarged again after 2010. We also look at Japan's nuclear power program and the plans in developing Asia, on which some useful arrangements for regional cooperation can hopefully be built. We devote the final section to nuclear power issues in the area of Central and Eastern Europe and the former Soviet Union.

This chapter is a bridge to our final chapter on the long-term environmental challenge and the transition from fossil fuels. It may be in this long-term, sustainable development context that nuclear power will make its greatest contribution to energy security. A world energy supply calculation by the Japan Institute of Energy Economics predicts that most of new energy demand in the twenty-first century will be met by burning coal. Yet if greenhouse gas emissions are limited to 1990 levels (as in the Rio conference commitments) because of the threat of global climate change, the use of coal will have to be restricted and the role of nuclear power dramatically increased, barring spectacular breakthroughs in wind, solar, hydro/geothermal, or industrial biomass energy sources.

A. UNITED STATES

The United States has the largest commercial nuclear energy program in the world, with 104 reactors in operation generating over 20 percent of the country's electricity. Nuclear energy enjoyed strong growth during the 1960s and 1970s when utilities faced the prospect of a countrywide annual growth rate in electricity demand between 7 and 8 percent. Concerns about energy security, as a result of the first oil shock, buoyed the prospects for nuclear energy. The 1979 Three Mile Island nuclear plant incident, however, began a reversal of its fortunes. Reductions in electricity demand growth, associated delays in project schedules, increasing construction costs, and a more stringent regulatory environment weakened the utilities' desire to construct additional nuclear plants. No new plants have been ordered since 1978.

We think the expansion of nuclear power is an important energy option for the United States to maintain into the twenty-first century. If this is to be case, there are two specific issues facing the nuclear industry that have to be addressed: (1) finding a solution to the problem of long-term storage of waste; and (2) ensuring that nuclear energy is an economically viable choice.

The single largest challenge facing the nuclear industry in the United States is the problem of long-term storage of spent nuclear fuel and other high-level radioactive wastes from commercial nuclear power installations. Until the 1970s, it was assumed that spent fuel would be reprocessed.[1] In 1977, President Carter, noting proliferation and economic concerns, indefinitely deferred the reprocessing of spent fuels and decided the United States would permanently dispose of spent fuel and other high-level radioactive waste in sealed steel canisters in underground repositories, commonly referred to as deep geological disposal.

Only in 1982 was major legislation passed governing the development of a scientifically, technically, and politically acceptable system for managing high-level radioactive wastes. The Nuclear Waste Policy Act (NWPA) of 1982 set forth the procedure for the selection of two repository sites and assigned the responsibility for the project to the Department of Energy (DOE). The NWPA specified a 1998 date for the start of waste acceptance and required the DOE to procure the hardware and develop the procedures and institutional arrangements for a transportation system that would carry the wastes from the various nuclear utilities to the final storage site. In 1987, the Nuclear Waste Policy Amendments Act directed the Secretary of Energy to "provide for an orderly phase-out of site specific activities at all candidate sites other than the Yucca Mountain site." Although still being studied to determine its geological suitability as a repository, the Yucca Mountain site, located in the state of Nevada, has become the country's only prospective site for the permanent disposal of spent fuel and other high-level radioactive wastes.

The opening of the permanent repository has been plagued by numerous political, legal and technical delays. Progress is being made. A tunnel of approximately two miles has been completed. Preliminary experiments testing the technical and environmental feasibility of the site have been positive. The new target date for completion is 2010. The DOE remains committed to completing the Yucca Mountain site.

The need to add spent fuel storage capacity is becoming increasingly urgent. Storage pools at some nuclear power plants are already filled to capacity, and about three-quarters of today's operating plants will face this dilemma over the next 20 years. The

---

[1]When nuclear fuel can no longer sustain a nuclear chain reaction, the irradiated or "spent" fuel rods are removed from the reactor. After a few years of cooling down, the spent fuel can be reprocessed to separate uranium and plutonium from other actinides and fission products. The spent fuel is dissolved in nitric acid, and uranium and plutonium are separated in a chemical process. The recovered uranium and plutonium are then ready to be re-introduced into the nuclear fuel cycle in a combined form known as mixed-oxide fuel which can be used in existing light water reactors. The rest (other actinides, fission products and impurities) constitutes high-level radioactive waste. The high-level waste is transformed into forms fit for disposal, such as vitrified waste.

slow-down in construction and various delays at the Yucca Mountain site have led to several proposals originating from Congress for the development of an interim monitored storage facility (MRS). The MRS facility, it is proposed, would be used until the long-term site is operational.

The economics of nuclear energy, compared with other energy choices, will determine whether or not the United States will replace the existing generation of nuclear power plants. The fuel itself, enriched uranium, is not the primary cost. More important are the costs of construction, storage of spent fuel, and decommissioning. If the regulatory environment is improved to the point where plants can be constructed within a relatively short period of time (similar to Japan which takes on average 5-7 years), the economics will be improved. At present, the economics point toward greater use of natural gas for electrical generation. The advancements in design, efficiency and operation of combined cycle turbines are making gas the fuel of choice for expanding capacity. In the post-2010 era, however, when utilities will be faced with expanding base-load capacity as a result of the retirement/decommissioning of coal-fired and nuclear plants, the arguments may turn toward nuclear energy. Improving the regulatory environment for the construction of a new generation of nuclear reactors is of critical importance. The Nuclear Regulatory Commission has in recent years established more streamlined licensing procedures and expedited the licensing process for pre-approved standard designs. The NRC has issued a new procedure for applying to extend the licenses of nuclear plants, now set at 40 years. The new NRC extension, if granted, would extend the life of current nuclear plants for another 20 years.

Although not directly related to the commercial nuclear energy program, the management and disposal of surplus weapons plutonium from dismantled nuclear weapons is emerging as a key issue in the nuclear debate in the United States. Two studies published by the National Academy of Sciences set out three options for dealing with the surplus weapons plutonium, with some preference for the first: (1) conversion to mixed-oxide fuel (MOX) for burning in existing light water reactors; (2) vitrification; and (3) burial in deep bore holes.[2] The American Nuclear Society convened a panel

---

[2]National Academy of Sciences, *Management and Disposition of Excess Weapons Plutonium* (Washington, DC: National Academy Press, 1994). National Academy of Sciences, *Management and Disposition of Excess Weapons Plutonium: Reactor Related Options* (Washington, DC: National Academy Press, 1995).

of international experts which likewise concluded that using the surplus weapons plutonium in commercial light water reactors represented the fastest and most effective method of disposal.[3] A final decision has not been made.

B. CANADA

Canada has developed a successful nuclear energy program based on the unique CANDU reactor design, which uses fuel channels instead of a pressure vessel and natural uranium instead of enriched uranium. The country has twenty-two nuclear reactors in operation, accounting for 18 percent of total electricity generation. Ontario Hydro, Canada's largest electrical utility, operates twenty of the reactors. The remaining two are managed by Hydro-Quebec and the New Brunswick Electric Power Company.

Faced with surplus capacity, none of the Canadian utilities plans to build additional nuclear plants. Maintaining and upgrading existing plants will be the principal activity for the foreseeable future. The poor prospects on the domestic market have encouraged Atomic Energy of Canada Limited to become active in the international market. CANDU reactors are in operation or are under consideration for construction in several Asian countries, including India, Pakistan, Indonesia, the Republic of Korea, and China. The CANDU reactor has an impressive record of safety and reliability.

Given its abundance of uranium (Canada is the world's leading producer and exporter of uranium), Canada has no plans to reprocess its spent fuel. Similar to the United States, Canada has adopted the "once through" fuel cycle with plans to develop a deep geological repository.[4] AECL has conducted a 16-year research program into the possibility of disposing the waste in crystalline igneous rock of the Canadian shield. According to AECL, both the disposal technology and the system to evaluate its safety have been demonstrated to the extent reasonably achievable in a generic research program. There are adequate storage facilities at all the

---

[3]American Nuclear Society, *Protection and Management of Plutonium*, Special Panel Report (La Grange Park, Illinois: American Nuclear Society Inc., 1995).

[4]The "nuclear fuel cycle" starts with the mining of natural uranium ore and proceeds through milling, conversion to uranium hexaflouride gas, enrichment, fuel fabrication, irradiation in a reactor, removal, storage, and disposition as waste or through reprocessing and recycling as fresh nuclear fuel. The "once through" fuel cycle involves storage and disposal of spent nuclear fuel, while the "closed" fuel cycle involves reprocessing of spent nuclear fuel and recycling into fresh fuel.

nuclear plants; consequently, AECL feels no urgency to dispose of the waste and does not plan to open a repository before 2025.

C. OECD EUROPE

Nuclear energy is an important component of OECD Europe's energy mix. Developed in large part because of an increasing dependence on imported oil, the nuclear industry has achieved a prominent position in electricity generation in several countries, as shown in Table 2. However, problems of public acceptance, of economics, and of the back-end of the nuclear fuel cycle have made nuclear energy's future uncertain.

TABLE 2
Nuclear Power Plants in Operation in OECD Europe (1994)

	Number of Operable Reactors	Number of Reactors Under Construction	Percentage of Electricity Generated by Nuclear
Belgium	7	0	56
Finland	4	0	29
France	56	4	75
Germany	21	0	29
Netherlands	2	0	5
Spain	9	0	35
Sweden	12	0	51
Switzerland	5	0	37
United Kingdom	34	1	26
TOTAL	**150**	**5**	**38 ***

Source: Nuclear Energy Agency, OECD
*unweighted average

France is the only exception in OECD Europe. There, nuclear energy continues to enjoy strong political and public backing. The country ranks first in the world in terms of per capita installed nuclear capacity. Approximately 75 percent of France's electricity is supplied from fifty-six reactors in service at eighteen sites. Currently, nuclear energy enjoys a 25 percent cost advantage (although this advantage is declining) over coal and gas-fired power. Unlike the United States and Canada, France has adopted the "closed fuel cycle" and reprocesses its spent fuel to recover and recycle uranium and plutonium. The recovered uranium and plutonium are converted into mixed-oxide fuel, which typical commercial light water reactors can use in one-third of their cores without major modification. EDF has plans to use MOX fuel in twenty-eight of its reactors; seven do so now.

EDF expects nuclear energy to retain its cost advantage even as its plants age and major components are replaced. Although EDF has not placed any new orders, it will proceed to construct four new plants. Framatome is designing the next generation of reactors—the European pressurized water reactor (EPWR)—in partnership with Siemens of Germany. This new generation of reactors is to replace the existing pressurized water reactors after 2010. The absence of new orders in France, as with the Canadian nuclear industry, has made the French active participants in the expanding Asian nuclear energy market.

Compagnie Générale des Matières Nucléaires (COGEMA)[5] operates the country's principal reprocessing facility at La Hague. There are also two MOX fuel fabrication plants in service at Cadarache and Marcoule. Approximately two-thirds of France's reprocessing work on spent fuel comes from domestic reactors, with the remainder coming from foreign customers who are returned the high-level radioactive waste and MOX fuel.

Despite its broad acceptance of nuclear energy, France has encountered unexpected opposition in siting a long-term waste repository. Late in 1991, the French Parliament passed legislation containing three key provisions on nuclear waste disposal. First, over 15 years, several concurrent research efforts are to be conducted, including an examination of geological disposal and of waste storage reduction methods. Second, the French waste management agency was given greater autonomy from the agency responsible for developing the nuclear industry. And third, a policy of openness with the public was initiated to help alleviate widespread concerns about high-level radioactive waste disposal. Because the research is to continue until around 2007, the French do not anticipate that a repository will be available until 2020, or beyond.[6]

The United Kingdom entered the nuclear field early, opening the world's first industrial-scale nuclear generating station at Calder Hall

---

[5]Framatome and Compagnie Générale des Matières Nucléaires are subsidiaries of the Commissariat à l'Energie Atomique (CEA), the French Atomic Energy Commission.
[6]Most of France's spent fuel is stored first at reactor sites in pools for about a year and then in facilities located at the reprocessing plants until it is reprocessed.

in 1956. Today, nuclear energy generates approximately 26 percent of the country's electricity. Thirty-four nuclear reactors are operated by three utilities—British Nuclear Fuels (BNFL), Nuclear Electric, and Scottish Nuclear Limited. BNFL, which is a government-owned entity, manages the Thermal Oxide Reprocessing Plant at Sellafield. The facility has been designed to reprocess spent fuel from both Advanced Gas-Cooled Reactors and pressurized water reactors. The plant serves both domestic and international clients, but is more reliant on its foreign customers.

In May 1995, the UK government announced that part of the nuclear industry would be privatized. The government concluded that the six older MAGNOX power stations would be kept in the public sector under the control of BNFL, since they will not generate enough money over their remaining lives. The more modern plants, operated by Nuclear Electric and Scottish Nuclear Limited and consisting of newer gas-cooled and pressurized water reactors, will be sold.

Long-term disposal of high-level radioactive waste is to be accomplished in a deep geological repository. A decision on a site, however, will not be made in the near future. The United Kingdom has a relatively low volume of high-level radioactive waste, all of which can easily be stored. The British believe storage offers the technical advantages of allowing the radioactivity to decay and the waste to cool.

In Germany, the government maintains that nuclear power is an important part of Germany's energy mix and asserts that nuclear power must be maintained as an energy option in the twenty-first century. It generates approximately 29 percent of the country's electricity. The German public's antipathy to nuclear energy is hardening. The 1986 Chernobyl disaster mobilized anti-nuclear forces in the country, including the Social Democratic Party which supports phasing out nuclear energy. If nuclear energy is to continue in Germany, new plants must begin to be constructed toward the end of the century to replace the older plants.

Reprocessing had been initially considered a part of the German fuel cycle and German utilities had contracted with both COGEMA in France and BNFL in the United Kingdom to reprocess spent fuel. But developments over the past several years—including demonstrations and other expressions of public opposition—have severely limited the future of reprocessing in Germany. A 1994 amendment to Germany's Atomic Act, the law originally requiring German utilities to reprocess their spent fuel, allows utilities the option of disposing their spent fuel by geological storage. As for a long-term geological disposal site, testing has been carried out at a salt formation near the town of Gorleben. If the site proves satisfactory, Germany plans to begin depositing high-level radioactive waste for final disposal in 2008.

In other parts of Europe, the prospects for nuclear power remain poor. Spain does not have any plans to expand its nuclear program, nor do Belgium, Finland, the Netherlands, or Sweden. Italy abandoned its nuclear program following the Chernobyl accident and has no plans to restart it. All these countries face similar challenges in finding a solution to the long-term disposal of their high-level radioactive waste. Apart from France, the European nuclear industry has few prospects in its home market. Its principal challenge, in the short-term, will be maintaining existing plants and continuing its exemplary safety record.

Several developments will need to come together if nuclear energy is to re-emerge in Europe in the post-2010 period: strong growth in demand for electricity, greater public acceptance, and the emergence of global climate change as a key determinant of energy policy.

D. JAPAN

Japan has the third largest civilian nuclear energy program in the world after the United States and France. Much of the rationale for Japan's strong nuclear program lies in the fact that it is a country with relatively few indigenous energy resources—relying for over 80 percent of its primary energy needs on foreign sources. As shown in Figure 17, nuclear energy has played a key role since 1973 in constraining dependence on foreign energy sources in Japan's electricity generation sector. The environment is another underlying reason for developing a strong nuclear program. Nuclear power is an integral part of the government's objective of stabilizing carbon dioxide emissions on a per capita basis in 2000 and beyond, at about the same level as 1990.

At the end of 1995, there were fifty nuclear power stations in operation in Japan. Total installed nuclear capacity was measured at 41.3 gigawatts (GWe). Approximate development targets for installed nuclear capacity are 45 GWe in 2000 and 70 GWe in 2010, although difficulty in siting may curtail this program. The Japanese government's target of having nuclear energy provide approximately 40 percent of electrical generation by 2010 will require the addition of over fifteen nuclear reactors.

FIGURE 17
Electricity Production in Japan

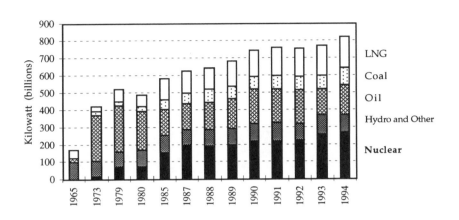

Source: Ministry of International Trade and Industry

Meeting this supply target represents a substantial challenge to both the government and the country's electric power companies. To secure the desired capacity, efforts are being focused on ensuring a continued high level of safety, improving plant reliability, reinforcing maintenance standards to cope with aging facilities, and studying waste management and disposal methods. As with many other countries, the principal challenge is gaining the public's acceptance of nuclear energy.

The importance of nuclear energy is further underlined by the long-term planning that the Japanese government and electric utilities are undertaking to develop a fully closed nuclear fuel cycle. This long-term strategy is being carried out with future generations in mind—the goal being to secure for them a safe, reliable, and environmentally sensitive fuel source in the twenty-first century. This program includes the reprocessing of spent fuel to recover uranium and plutonium to be reused in existing commercial light water reactors in the form of MOX fuel and continuing the development of fast breeder reactor technology. Fast breeder reactor technology is expected to become commercially viable around 2030.[7]

---

[7]The fast breeder reactor generates more fuel (plutonium) than it consumes during operation. This would provide Japan with an almost inexhaustible supply of energy.

From the perspective of maximizing national energy resources, it is not enough to replace oil with nuclear energy. It is also important to make the nuclear energy program as self-sufficient as possible by reprocessing spent fuel and recycling plutonium into MOX fuel and by commercializing fast breeder reactor technology. From a waste management perspective as well, the closed fuel cycle makes sense for Japan. First, reprocessing of spent fuel reduces by 40 percent the volume of high-level radioactive waste. And second, since reusable uranium and plutonium (both with a long half-life) are extracted during the reprocessing, the radioactivity of the remaining waste fades away more quickly.[8]

Currently, Japan is preparing to use the uranium and plutonium recovered from spent fuel (in the form of MOX fuel) in several of its light water reactors. In the country's *Long-Term Program for Research, Development, and Utilization of Nuclear Energy,* as revised in June 1994, the plan is for MOX fuel to be used gradually in several light water reactors toward the end of the century. As Japan does not yet possess a domestic commercial reprocessing plant, Japanese utility companies have signed contracts with COGEMA in France and BNFL in the United Kingdom to reprocess their spent fuel. The recovered plutonium and uranium is being converted into MOX fuel. The MOX fuel and resulting high-level radioactive waste (vitrified residue) is then returned to Japan.[9] The use of MOX fuel represents an important step toward establishing Japan's closed fuel cycle. It will both play an important role as an energy resource for Japan's nuclear power program and allow for the development of technologies and infrastructure necessary for the eventual commercialization of fast breeder reactor technology.

In an effort to increase Japan's domestic reprocessing capabilities, Japan Nuclear Fuel Limited (JNFL) was created in 1982. Established in large part by Japan's electric utility companies, JNFL has been charged with constructing a domestic reprocessing facility in northern Japan in Aomori Prefecture. The Aomori nuclear facility, when completed, will include a uranium enrichment facility, a low-level

---

[8]Development of the closed fuel cycle is instrumental to Japan's strategy of long-term storage of high-level radioactive waste. High-level radioactive waste separated from spent fuel at reprocessing facilities will cool down during 30 to 50 years of storage, and will ultimately be disposed of in deep geological repositories. The entity to implement the disposal project for high-level radioactive waste will be established around 2000. The start of repository operations is foreseen sometime after 2030, but no later than the 2040s.

[9]In April 1995, the first return shipment of vitrified high-level radioactive waste was successfully returned from Europe. Upon arrival at the Japanese port of Mutsu-Ogawara, the vitrified high-level radioactive waste was taken to the waste management facility in Rokkashomura for storage.

radioactive waste disposal center, and a reprocessing facility. The uranium enrichment facility and low-level radioactive waste disposal center have been completed and commenced operations in March 1992 and December 1992 respectively. The reprocessing plant is scheduled to begin operation in 2003.

The development of fast breeder reactor technology remains the long-term goal of Japan's nuclear energy program. Through a series of experimental, prototype, and demonstration reactors, Japan hopes to improve its fast breeder technology. The experimental reactor "Joyo" has been operational since 1977. In April 1994, the prototype reactor "Monju" reached criticality (achieved a sustained chain reaction). There are plans to begin construction of a demonstration reactor sometime after 2000. A sodium leak at the Monju reactor in December 1995 resulted in a temporary shut-down. Although not considered a serious technical problem, this incident has created a difficult public acceptance challenge and could delay the long-term program somewhat. Nevertheless, the government and the country's electric power companies remain committed to the development of fast breeder technology. As with any new technology, its costs are high, but so is the cost of maintaining a military presence in the Gulf region to secure oil for America and the world. And Japan's long-term nuclear program contributes to collective energy security.

E. CHINA AND DEVELOPING EAST ASIA

For the rapidly developing countries of East Asia, nuclear power is viewed as an important part of meeting long-term energy demands. Except for China, most countries lack indigenous energy resources and are dependent on imports to fuel their economies. Increasing dependence on foreign sources of energy, along with the world's fastest growing demand for electricity, is leading several countries to consider or expand existing nuclear power programs. Another argument in favor of developing commercial nuclear facilities relates to reducing the growing emissions from combustion of fossil fuels. Given concerns over global climate change, acid deposition, and urban pollution, nuclear energy (given adherence to strict safety guidelines) has some important advantages relative to coal and oil-fired electricity generating plants.

China has the most ambitious plans to expand its nuclear energy program. Meeting the increasing demand for electricity, which has more than doubled in the past 10 years, is the primary reason for its aggressive long-term nuclear energy strategy. The three civilian nuclear reactors now operating in China began commercial operations in the first half of 1994. The Qinshan 1 reactor (288 MWe), which first went critical in 1991, is based on domestic technology. DaiaBay 1 (935 MWe) and DaiaBay 2 (935 Mwe) are Framatome plants, with much of their output exported to Hong Kong.

The timetables for expanding China's nuclear energy program stretch out over decades. Speaking before the Pacific Basin Nuclear Conference in May 1995, Chen Zhaobo, Vice Minister of China's Atomic Energy Authority, stated that China plans to install approximately 350 GWe of nuclear capacity by 2050. Table 3 illustrates the various projections of future installed nuclear generating capacity in China.

TABLE 3
Estimates for Chinese Installed Nuclear Capacity (MWe)

	1994	2000	2010	2020	2030	2050
China Electric Industry Corp.	2,100	3,000				
China Energy Institute	2,100	2,100	15,000			
China Nuclear Corp.	2,100	3,500	20,000/ 25,000	64,000/ 84,000	135,000/ 170,000	300,000/ 350,000
Hydro Energy Institute	2,100	2,100	15,000/ 20,000	35,000/ 60,000		
IEA	2,100	2,100	10,700/ 15,000			
Yamaji	2,100	2,100/ 2,700	18,100/ 25,700			

China will face many difficulties in expanding its nuclear program. It will be forced to raise the necessary capital, train operators, and establish a regulatory regime similar to ones in Trilateral countries. It is unlikely China will reach 350 GWe of installed capacity by 2050.

Nevertheless, the estimates indicate the seriousness with which China views nuclear energy. Faced with declining prospects for nuclear energy in OECD countries, foreign companies are actively pursuing the Chinese market.

As part of its nuclear expansion program, China is embarking upon the development of a closed fuel cycle. A pilot reprocessing plant is being constructed to handle civilian spent fuel and there are plans to build a larger plant around 2010. In the interim, spent fuel is being stored at the reactor sites. It will eventually be transported to the Lanzhou Nuclear Fuel Complex when it is completed toward the end of the century.

Faced with increasing reliance upon imported energy resources, especially oil imports from the Gulf region, other East Asian countries are also planning to expand or develop the nuclear energy option. South Korea established its nuclear energy program in the 1950s and now has ten nuclear reactors in operation generating 35 percent of its electricity. The Korean Electric Power Corporation plans to have twenty-seven nuclear reactors in operation by 2010.

Taiwan's rapid industrialization has likewise entailed an increased demand for power. The state-owned utility, Taipower, is committed to expanding its nuclear energy program, despite the efforts of anti-nuclear groups which have made site selection for new reactors more difficult. Taiwan has six reactors in operation, with an installed capacity of almost 5 gigawatts.

As these countries expand nuclear power generation, a number of issues will have to be addressed. These include developing a culture of safety regarding the construction and operation of nuclear plants; ensuring adherence to nuclear non-proliferation guidelines[10]; implementing a policy for dealing with spent fuel, whether that be long-term geological disposal or reprocessing; and entering into multilateral and/or bilateral agreements which help address the aforementioned issues.

With the region's most advanced nuclear power program, Japan can play a key role in these countries developing safe and efficient nuclear power programs. With its extensive experience in design, construction, operation and maintenance of plants, and management of spent fuel, Japan has much to offer these countries. One idea is for the countries of the region to establish cooperatives arrangements that could lead to the creation of an Asian Atomic Energy Community (ASIATOM), though ASIATOM is a concept yet to be defined. Without the history of the

---

[10]We welcome the agreement negotiated with North Korea, and urge more Trilateral countries in Europe to join with Japan, the United States, Canada, and other countries in the Korean Peninsula Energy Development Organization (KEDO).

European Coal and Steel Community or the context of security-oriented organizations like WEU or even CSCE, creation of East Asia-wide arrangements only for the nuclear fuel cycle will require approaches that are quite different from EURATOM. The subject is being considered seriously, but as yet without any viable proposal. Presumably ASIATOM would promote transparency, the safe operation of nuclear facilities, and the safe disposal of nuclear waste material. The coordinated management and inspection of plutonium stocks held by all member states, including Japan, would be an important part of this regional framework.

F. CENTRAL AND EASTERN EUROPE
AND THE FORMER SOVIET UNION

There are sixty-six nuclear reactors in operation in Central and Eastern Europe and the area of the former Soviet Union. Russia and Ukraine account for two-thirds of the region's nuclear plants. As shown in Table 4, both countries are constructing additional nuclear generating capacity; however, the transition from centralized to

TABLE 4
Nuclear Power Plants in Operation in Central and Eastern Europe and the Former Soviet Union (1994)

	Number of Operable Reactors	Number of Reactors Under Construction	Percentage of Electricity Generated by Nuclear
Bulgaria	6	0	46
Armenia	0	2	0
Kazakhstan	1	0	1
Russia	29	10	11
Ukraine	15	7	34
Czech Republic	4	2	28
Hungary	4	0	44
Lithuania	2	0	76
Romania	0	5	0
Slovak Republic	4	4	49
Slovenia	1	0	38
TOTAL	**66**	**30**	**30 ***

Source: Nuclear Energy Agency, OECD
*unweighted average

market-oriented economies is making it difficult for many of these projects to be completed. Of greater importance is the need to improve safety standards and shut down unsafe reactors.

G-7 countries have been actively involved in nuclear reactor safety issues in Russia and the Newly Independent States. The principal concern has been the fifteen Chernobyl-design reactors (RBMK 1000) and the four VVER 440/230 reactors currently in operation.[11] G-7 countries have urged that all these reactors be shut down. Another accident on the scale of Chernobyl would have severe consequences for nuclear power worldwide.

It is difficult to deal with these safety concerns. The shutting down of unsafe reactors has to be put in the context of plans to provide replacement power. These plans in turn have to be put in the context of overall economic (and energy sector) restructuring, to attract private investment that will be needed alongside whatever public funds Trilateral and other governments can provide.

In 1995, a Center for Strategic and International Studies (CSIS) Task Force released a report entitled Nuclear Energy Safety Challenges in the Former Soviet Union.[12] The report recommends a plan which would require at least 10 years of effort—a "decade of stabilization"—and cost between $20-30 billion. Its major elements are: (1) support for cost-effective safety improvements, training, and management during continuing operation, without explicit shut-down dates; (2) options for electricity generation within the context of energy policies worked out between the host governments and the G-7 countries; (3) acceptance that the oldest reactors must be shut down as alternative electricity supply becomes available; and (4) a social safety net for displaced employees when nuclear reactors are shut down. The CSIS Task Force offered four approaches to provide the funds needed: (1) add surcharges to the monthly electricity bills of consumers in the EU and G-7 member-countries; (2) use the Russian stockpile of refined uranium as collateral for loans; (3) involve private foreign investors in constructing compensating generating capacity on a "build-operate-transfer" basis, if investment conditions are

---

[11]RBMK is an acronym for Reaktory Bolshoi Moshchnosti Kanalnye (high-power pressure tube reactors). VVER is an acronym for Vodo-Vodyannoy Energeticheskiy Reactor (water-cooled, water-moderated). The countries in which these type of reactors are in operation are: Russia, Ukraine, Lithuania, and Armenia.

[12]Center for Strategic and International Studies, *Nuclear Energy Safety Challenges in the Former Soviet Union,* A Consensus Report of the CSIS Congressional Study Group on Nuclear Energy Safety Challenges in the Former Soviet Union, chaired by James Schlesinger (Washington, DC: CSIS, 1995), pp. 1-4. The World Bank, together with the IEA, came up with similar conclusions in a joint report written upon request of the G-7 (at the Tokyo Summit, 1992).

sufficiently attractive; and (4) World Bank financing of electricity generating projects that would allow phase out of the oldest nuclear power plants.

In April 1996, the issue of nuclear safety was the subject of a special G-7 plus Russia and Ukraine Nuclear Summit in Moscow. The Summit in Moscow recognized the importance of nuclear energy for Russia, Ukraine and other Newly Independent States. It recognized the need for safety and for security-related technical (and possibly financial) assistance. The Summit has not yet produced concrete proposals, but it has produced the important psychological result that the G-7 countries now fully recognize that Russia is a serious partner in the nuclear field, beyond mere technical "assistance" programs. This new partnership heralds a better working relationship in this area.

VIII. THE ENVIRONMENTAL CHALLENGE

The third face of energy security, the "sustainable development" face, was not a concern for most of this century. It has rapidly gained salience in recent decades and now, in the 1990s, is probably the most visible of all three faces of energy security in the broad policy debate in our countries, especially in Europe and Canada. These issues carry us well beyond 2010.

We divide the energy-related environmental challenge into three parts. First is the threat of global climate change, which reinforces the global context in which the Trilateral countries must work to maintain energy security. The most dramatic step taken by many Trilateral governments to address this threat is their commitment under the 1992 Framework Convention on Climate Change to reduce anthropogenic greenhouse gas emissions by 2000 or 2005 to 1990 levels. The very large gap between this commitment and any available means for implementation is reminiscent of the oil import targets committed to by our governments in 1979 in the midst of the second oil crisis. The political salience of the challenge has brought forth a sweeping commitment that governments do not know how to implement. As it becomes clear that the public expectations aroused by these commitments regarding greenhouse gas emissions will not be met, the credibility of Trilateral governments may be further diminished. Trilateral policymakers have many years of innovative work before them in elaborating more discriminating "framework conditions" which make use of the virtues of markets while slowing the growth in emissions of carbon dioxide and other greenhouse gases.

The regional environmental challenge of acid deposition is taken up in the second of the following sections. The science of "acid rain" and other acid depositions is less uncertain and the policy tools more refined than in the case of global climate change. The problem of acid deposition is growing dramatically in rapidly industrializing Asia. The progress that Trilateral countries have made in this area will hopefully shorten the learning curve among policymakers and others in developing Asia. The story is similar with regard to the challenge of urban air pollution, discussed in the third section.

The 50 years since the end of World War II have been an unusual period in human history. The world's population doubled and very rapid progress in science and technology brought about major changes in human society. There were remarkable changes in standards of living, in the lethal power of weapons, and in the speed and ease with which people can communicate and move around. The abundant supply of oil from the Middle East was one important factor in this "progress." As we look out over the next half century to 2050, we cannot assume that it will be an extrapolation of the past half century. We just do not know if and how science and technology will continue to progress, whether abundant energy will be available, or whether and how the environmental limitations of the earth's bearing power may be over-stretched.

Thus, energy projections out to 2050 are necessarily speculative. We do assume that the world's population will increase by several billion, an increase overwhelmingly concentrated outside Trilateral countries. Even if per capita energy use remains constant, the population increase alone would significantly increase world energy use. Hopefully per capita incomes in today's developing countries will increase many times over in the course of the next five decades. We are not certain which technologies ultimately will meet energy demands over the long-term, but know that they should be clean, secure, and economically competitive. A number of breakthroughs are possible in the transportation sector, which will demand an increasing portion of the world's oil production. Other technologies will improve the efficiency of electricity generation. The final section of this chapter briefly sketches some of the medium-term and long-term technological options which may be critical for the third face of energy security to be addressed successfully.

A. GLOBAL CLIMATE CHANGE

Concern over the ways human activities can alter the global atmosphere has increased dramatically over the past 25 years.[1] Much

---

[1]The authors recognize that another important global atmospheric issue is stratospheric ozone depletion. In 1974, a landmark scientific paper pointed out that chlorine-containing substances called chlorofluorocarbons (more commonly referred to as CFCs) pose a threat to the ozone layer. The underlying reason for concern is that ozone is the only gas in the atmosphere that limits the most harmful solar ultraviolet radiation reaching the surface of the earth. An increase in the amount of ultraviolet radiation reaching the earth's surface would have potential harmful effects on human health and on the productivity of aquatic and terrestrial ecosystems. The Vienna Convention (1985) and the Montreal Protocol on Substances that Deplete the Ozone Layer (1987), as amended, require industrial countries to phase out production of CFCs by 1996—a target industrialized countries are meeting.

of the attention has focused on how human activities affect the natural concentration of greenhouse gases in the global atmosphere.[2] The combustion of fossil fuels results in emissions of all three of the major greenhouse gases: carbon dioxide, nitrous oxide and methane. Carbon dioxide has received the most attention, representing the largest share of global greenhouse gas emissions from human-induced sources. Many experts believe that rising atmospheric concentrations of greenhouse gases resulting from human activities (e.g., energy use, land change, and industrial processes) could result in global climate change entailing severe detrimental economic and ecological effects.

The first broad assessment of global climate change emerged in 1990 when the Intergovernmental Panel on Climate Change (IPCC), jointly sponsored by the World Meteorological Organization and the United Nations Environment Programme, issued its first report. The study involved the efforts of several hundred leading atmospheric scientists from many countries. The IPCC was established under the auspices of the United Nations in late 1988 to accumulate available scientific research on climate change and to provide advice to policymakers. Among the IPCC's conclusions in the 1990 study were that global mean temperatures will likely rise at a rate of 0.3 °C per decade if current emission trends of greenhouse gases continue, a faster global warming rate than any of the last 10,000 years. At this rate, temperatures would rise by about 1 °C by 2025 and 3 °C before the end of the next century. In the same time frame, sea levels would rise by approximately 65 centimeters.

Uncertainty continues to surround the theory of global climate change regarding the extent and speed of such change, its overall effects and regional distribution, and the cost and effectiveness of efforts to prevent, slow down, or adapt to the change.[3] In spite of this

---

[2]The natural greenhouse effect refers to the phenomenon by which the Earth's atmosphere traps infrared radiation or heat. Gases that cause the greenhouse effect are water vapor (H_2O), carbon dioxide (CO_2), methane (CH_4), nitrous oxide (N_2O), and halocarbons (such as CFC-11 and CFC-12). With the exception of halocarbons, most greenhouse gases occur naturally. Without the heat trapping properties of the greenhouse gases, which make up no more than 1 or 2 percent of the Earth's atmosphere, the average temperature of the Earth would be similar to Mars (-16 °C).

[3]In December 1995, the IPCC released a broad review of global climate change research since its 1990 report. The 1995 review concluded that "the balance of evidence suggests a discernible human influence on global climate change." If no changes are made in emissions of greenhouse gases, the IPCC projects an increase in global mean surface air temperature relative to 1990 of about 2 °C by 2100. The projected warming is one-third lower than the "best estimate" in 1990. This is primarily due to lower emission scenarios (particularly for CO_2 and CFCs), the inclusion of the cooling effect of sulfate aerosols, and improvements in the treatment of the carbon cycle. According to the IPCC, this rate of warming would still be the greatest experienced in the last 10,000 years. See Intergovernmental Panel on Climate Change (IPCC), *IPCC Second Assessment Synthesis of Scientific-Technical Information Relevant to Interpreting Article 2 of the UN Framework Convention on Climate Change* (Geneva: World Meteorological Organization/United Nations Environment Programme, 1995).

uncertainty, the magnitude of the risk led more than 150 countries to sign the Framework Convention on Climate Change (the Convention) in Rio de Janeiro on May 4, 1992. The process had been initiated by the United Nations in 1990 when it established the Intergovernmental Negotiating Committee for a Framework Convention on Climate Change (INC). The INC hosted a series of negotiating sessions that culminated in the signing of the Convention in Rio. The objective of the Rio Convention is to ". . . achieve stabilization of the greenhouse gas concentrations in the atmosphere at a level that would prevent dangerous anthropogenic interference with the climate system" (Article 2). The Convention, as it emerged from the negotiations, is based on the concept of voluntary commitments by signatories to implement the objectives of the Convention. The Convention became legally binding in March 1994 when the required fifty signatories had ratified it.[4]

The majority of Trilateral countries have adopted specific targets to limit carbon dioxide or total greenhouse gas emissions; about half have adopted the target to stabilize and/or reduce anthropogenic emissions of carbon dioxide by 2000 or 2005 to levels prevailing in an earlier year (in most cases 1990). Parties are required to report to the Convention Secretariat on their projected greenhouse gas emissions and the policies and measures they propose to put in place to mitigate emissions, as well as to make specific estimates of the effects that actual and planned measures will have on anthropogenic emissions.

Most governments will be relying heavily on energy-related measures to meet their commitments. Increased efficiency in the use of fossil fuels is being emphasized. Switching to less carbon-intensive fuels, in particular to natural gas and renewables, is expected by many governments to make an important contribution to emission reductions.[5]

During the spring of 1995, the Conference of Parties under the Framework Convention held its first meeting in Berlin. The industrialized countries committed themselves to agree by 1997, when they will meet again in Tokyo, on targets for reducing greenhouse gas emissions beyond 2000. A pilot phase for "joint implementation" activities under the Convention was approved. Joint implementation, for instance, will encourage firms in developed countries to transfer technology and make investments that enable

---

[4]As of June 1995, more than 137 countries had ratified the Convention.
[5]The United States accounts for nearly half of OECD energy-related carbon dioxide emissions and Japan and Germany for about 10 percent each.

developing countries to reduce their emissions of greenhouse gases.[6] A framework for technology transfer was adopted and an OECD/IEA Climate Technology Initiative announced.

Although the political leaders of OECD countries have made commitments to stabilize their greenhouse gas emissions (at 1990 levels) by around 2000, these commitments will not be achieved. The necessary energy policies to meet these targets are not being implemented. It will take much more than increased energy efficiency to achieve these goals. In fact, projections by the GEMS Model indicate that energy-related carbon dioxide emissions in 2010 will be over 30 percent higher than the 1990 level. If the issue of global climate change is to be taken seriously over the long-term, a fundamental change will have to be made in the global energy structure, with increased reliance on non-fossil fuels such as nuclear and renewable energy resources.

The global context for maintaining energy security is starkly evident with regard to climate change. Within the next 15 years, greenhouse gas emissions from developing countries are expected to double, rising from 28 to 45 percent of the world total. India and China, which now produce less than one-third the emissions of OECD countries, will account for a larger increase in annual emissions from 1990 to 2010 than all OECD countries combined. The assumptions regarding population growth, economic growth and energy use in the developing world on which these projections are based may not be borne out over time, but to assume much less population growth and economic growth and much more progress on energy efficiency and use of non-fossil fuels is not warranted by current circumstances. Developing countries will have to be full participants along with Trilateral countries if global climate change is to be addressed in an adequate fashion.

B. ACID DEPOSITION

Acid deposition, either in a wet form (acid rain, snow, fog, and cloud vapors) or a dry form (acidic particulates and aerosols), occurs when large volumes of sulfur dioxide and nitrogen oxides are released from the combustion of fossil fuels. These gaseous oxides react with water

---

[6]More broadly, joint implementation refers to international arrangements whereby private industry, governmental entities and non-governmental organizations in one country undertake mitigation and sequestration jointly with entities in another.

in the air or on the surface of small particulates to produce sulfuric and nitric acids. Sulfur dioxide and nitrogen oxide emissions primarily originate from coal-burning electric power generation, base-metal smelting, oil and gas processing, and fuel combustion from vehicles.[7] Many stationary sources inject these gases high into the atmosphere, where most are converted to sulfate and nitrate particles and distributed downwind. If captured by prevailing winds, they may be transported as much as 1,000 kilometers before being deposited. Dry deposition usually occurs closer to the emission source.

Acid deposition can have severe effects on both terrestrial and aquatic ecosystems. Over time, as the soil loses its capacity to buffer the acid load, both soils and surface waters gradually acidify, disrupting the chemical and biological processes of the organisms that live there.[8] Sensitive aquatic species can decline rapidly as acidity disrupts their reproductive cycles. Increased acidity can also have pronounced effects on the nutrient balance available in the soil by causing the accelerated leaching of essential plant nutrients such as calcium, magnesium, and potassium ions. Higher soil acidity leads to increased levels of soluble aluminum, a plant toxin that damages fine roots and interferes with the uptake of remaining calcium and magnesium. Excessive levels of nitrogen from acid deposition can over-stimulate plant growth and exacerbate nutrient deficiencies. Forests in Central Europe receive four to eight times as much nitrogen through acid deposition as they need for growth.[9]

Transboundary acid deposition first became a major concern in the highly industrialized regions of Europe and North America during the 1970s and 1980s and is beginning to become evident in many areas of East Asia (see Map 3). Large scale forest decline in many parts of Europe is directly attributable to soil acidification. In the past 20 to 50 years, the soils in many of Europe's forests have become five to ten times more acidic. According to a recent analysis, about 75 percent of Europe's commercial forests suffer damaging levels of sulfur deposition, and 60 percent endure nitrogen depositions above their critical loads (the amount they can handle without harm). In

---

[7]Stationary sources are responsible for almost all human-caused sulfur dioxide emissions and approximately 35 percent of human-caused nitrogen oxides emissions. Vehicle traffic generates between 30 and 50 percent of total nitrogen oxide emissions in industrialized countries.

[8]The impact of acidity depends on the system's buffering capacity. For instance, if the soil in the watershed contains limestone or other substances that neutralize acidity, lakes acidify less rapidly.

[9]World Resources Institute, *World Resources 1992-93: A Guide to the Global Environment* (New York: Oxford University Press, 1992), p. 198.

MAP 3
Regional Acid Deposition

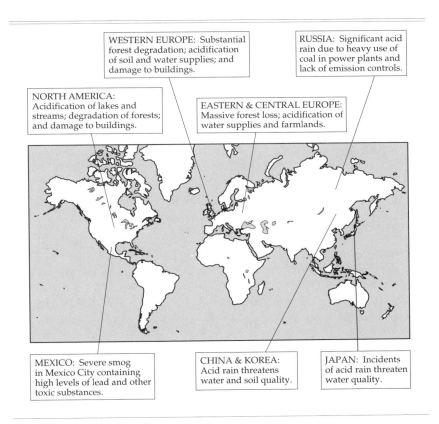

WESTERN EUROPE: Substantial forest degradation; acidification of soil and water supplies; and damage to buildings.

RUSSIA: Significant acid rain due to heavy use of coal in power plants and lack of emission controls.

NORTH AMERICA: Acidification of lakes and streams; degradation of forests; and damage to buildings.

EASTERN & CENTRAL EUROPE: Massive forest loss; acidification of water supplies and farmlands.

MEXICO: Severe smog in Mexico City containing high levels of lead and other toxic substances.

CHINA & KOREA: Acid rain threatens water and soil quality.

JAPAN: Incidents of acid rain threaten water quality.

Source: World Resources Institute

North America, the biggest problem has been the acidification of lakes and rivers, although forests have also been damaged.

Corrosion of stone and metal building materials and monuments has also become a serious problem in both Europe and North America. Increasing attention is being paid to the health effects of acid aerosols derived from the chemical transformation of sulfur dioxide and nitrogen oxides in the atmosphere. Mounting evidence suggests that acid aerosols may damage human health by contributing to respiratory problems such as bronchitis and asthma.

Combating the acid deposition problem requires regional

cooperation. In 1979, thirty-five countries from Europe and North America signed the Convention on Long-Range Transboundary Air Pollution. What was at first a relatively weak document has become an effective mechanism for reducing regional emissions. A protocol requiring a 30 percent reduction in sulfur dioxide emissions from 1980 levels by 1993 was adopted in 1985. A second protocol, mandating a cap on nitrogen oxide emissions at 1987 levels, was adopted in 1988. Immediately following this, members of the European Community further committed to 30 percent reductions in nitrogen oxide emissions by 1998. Substantial declines in sulfur dioxide emissions are being realized in Europe. Overall, sulfur dioxide emissions fell by more than 20 percent from 1980 to 1990. In several countries, where political momentum for pollution abatement is strong, greater reductions have been achieved. Reducing nitrogen oxide emissions has proven more difficult, and emission increases rather than declines have been the rule in all but a few countries.

In North America, the problem of acid deposition brought the United States and Canada together in a bilateral air accord (Canada/U.S. Air Quality Agreement) in addition to the associated Clean Air legislation in the two countries. The 1990 Clean Air Act in the United States requires that annual emissions of sulfur dioxide (approximately 20 million tons of sulfur dioxide emissions are emitted annually in the United States) be reduced by 10 million tons from 1980 levels. This legislation established an innovative market-based trading system that allows utilities to minimize the cost of complying with sulfur dioxide emission reduction requirements. The trading program encourages energy conservation and technological innovation.

Although acid deposition has received considerable attention in Europe and North America, recognition of the phenomenon is just beginning in Asia.[10] There is not yet the cross-national scientific or public constituency to address the problem. Available monitoring

---

[10]The World Bank and Asian Development Bank are funding a major research project studying the effects of acid deposition on Asia—the RAINS-ASIA program. The RAINS-ASIA program is a collaborative effort involving several research institutions in Asia, Europe and North America. Phase I of the project is to develop a methodology (the RAINS-ASIA Model) to assess the impacts of various acid rain emission reduction strategies. The goals of the project are: (1) to develop approaches that assist in formulating national and regional policies to address the rapidly emerging problem of atmospheric emissions in Asia; (2) to provide preliminary assessments needed to catalyze the process of inter-governmental policy dialogue on acid rain precursor emission control in Asia; and (3) to develop basic strategies for the World Bank, the Asian Development Bank, and other donor institutions concerning policy advice, institution building, and investment initiatives in the borrowing countries to implement the findings.

data show that the acidity of rainfall has been rising dramatically in some areas of the region—and it will continue to rise with Asia relying on fossil fuels for over 80 percent of its growing primary energy needs. Given that some of the ecosystems in Asia are similar to those found in Europe and North America, the impacts of acid deposition in Asia can be expected to be significant, especially for the agricultural and forestry industries.[11]

The effects are already evident in southern coastal China, the Korean peninsula, and Japan. If countermeasures are not taken, acid deposition in many areas will increase by more than a factor of five and exceed the levels observed in the most polluted areas in Central and Eastern Europe.[12] Because a large percentage of the acidifying compounds will be emitted from large energy facilities with high stacks, the effects will be widely spread. Table 5 shows the current and projected emissions of sulfur dioxide for Europe, North America and Asia. The total projected sulfur dioxide emissions for Asian countries in 2000 and 2010 far exceed North America and Europe combined.

TABLE 5
Current and Projected Sulfur Dioxide Emissions by Region
(metric tons)

	1990	2000	2010
Europe	38.0	22.0	14.0
North America	21.0	15.0	14.0
Asia	34.0	53.0	78.0
China	22.0	34.0	48.0
India	4.5	6.6	10.9
Other	7.5	12.4	19.1

Source: RAINS-ASIA Program

C. URBAN AIR POLLUTION

At the turn of the century, approximately 5 percent of the world's population lived in cities with populations over 100,000. Today, an

---

[11]Some experts have pointed out that acid deposition could severely impact China's agricultural productivity, threatening to turn China into a net importer of rice in the next century.
[12]Wes Foel et al, *RAINS-ASIA: An Assessment Model for Air Pollution in Asia*, Report on the World Bank Sponsored Project: "Acid Rain and Emission Reductions in Asia" (Washington, DC: World Bank, 1995).

estimated 45 percent, slightly more than 2.5 billion, live in urban centers. In recent years, the majority of this growth has been in developing countries. By 2025, the United Nations predicts, approximately five billion people, or 61 percent of the global population, will be living in cities.

A large percentage of these urban dwellers will be living with heavy industrial and vehicular air pollution. Usually generated by the combustion of fossil fuels, the degree of air pollution depends on pollution reduction efforts, choice of fuels, technologies available, climate, weather, and topography. Six pollutants are most serious: (1) *Suspended particulate matter* (SPM) includes smoke, soot, dust, and liquid droplets emitted from fuel combustion, industrial processes, or a number of natural sources. These can have especially toxic effects if they carry heavy metals or hydrocarbons. (2) *Sulfur dioxide* arises predominantly from the combustion of sulfur-containing fossil fuels, mostly coal. In addition to its role in acid deposition, sulfur dioxide can be a potent respiratory irritant. (3) *Nitrogen oxides* form when atmospheric oxygen and nitrogen, as well as the nitrogen contained in the fuel source, react at high temperatures. Nitrogen oxides are an important contributor to the formation of photochemical smog. (4) *Ozone* forms when nitrogen oxides, produced during fuel combustion, react with volatile organic compounds in the presence of sunlight.[13] The health effects of ozone are varied and can be severe. Symptoms include stinging eyes, coughing, and chest discomfort. (5) *Carbon monoxide* is created by the incomplete combustion of carbon-containing fuels. Vehicle exhaust accounts for nearly all of the carbon monoxide emitted in urban areas. Successful carbon dioxide reduction strategies rely chiefly on auto emission controls, such as catalytic converters. Reduction in carbon monoxide emissions has been successful in the developed world; however, most developing countries are experiencing increases in carbon monoxide levels as vehicle numbers and traffic congestion rise. (6) *Lead* is derived from fuel additives, metal smelters and, for the most part, leaded gasoline. Lead exposure has cumulative effects and can result in a variety of adverse health conditions. Prospects for global reduction in lead emissions are one of the few bright spots in the overall air pollution picture, at least in OECD countries. Reducing the permissible level of

---

[13]The sources for VOCs are many and varied. Vehicles, refineries, gas stations, and solvent sources such as dry cleaners, print shops, and house paints all contribute to the wide range of volatile compounds.

lead in petrol has been the primary means of reducing ambient lead concentrations. In many cities of the developing world, conversion to unleaded fuel is not yet complete.[14]

In 1992, the World Health Organization and the United Nations Environmental Programme joined forces to publish *Urban Air Pollution in the Megacities of the World*. Megacities are defined in the study as those urban areas that have more than ten million people or will have more than ten million by 2000, as estimated by the United Nations. The study covered twenty of the world's megacities (refer to Table 6). The study has its weaknesses. Real differences in methods,

TABLE 6
Status of Pollutants in the Megacities (1992)

City	Sulfur Dioxide	Suspended Particulate Matter	Lead	Carbon Dioxide	Nitrogen Oxide	Ozone
Bankok						
Beijing						
Bombay						
Buenos Aires						
Cairo						
Calcutta						
Delhi						
Djakarta						
Karachi						
London						
Los Angeles						
Manila						
Mexico City						
Moscow						
New York						
Rio de Janeiro						
Sao Paulo						
Seoul						
Shanghai						
Tokyo						

■ Serious pollution: WHO guidelines exceeded by more than a factor of two.
▒ Moderate to heavy pollution: WHO guidelines exceeded by up to a factor of two.
░ Low pollution: WHO guidelines normally met.
— No data available or insufficient data for assessment.

Sources: World Health Organization (WHO) and United Nations Environment Programme

[14]Op. cit., World Resources Institute, *World Resources 1992-93: A Guide to the Global Environment.*

concepts, standards, and calibration mark the reporting on various cities and countries. Nonetheless, the megacities study provides the first global look at numerous urban environments. Every city studied had at least one major pollutant that exceeded World Health Organization guidelines; fourteen cities had at least two, and seven cities had at least three.

D. MEDIUM-TERM AND LONG-TERM TECHNOLOGICAL OPTIONS

Holding in check the damage to the global, regional, and urban environments will require a combination of technical improvements and policy initiatives. Technological options are available and being implemented in various countries. In the electricity supply sector, switching to cleaner-burning fuels (either natural gas or low-sulfur coal) is one important and relatively simple option that would help reduce harmful emissions. Availability and cost are the greatest obstacles. The wider use of natural gas is almost certain to figure prominently in pollution control efforts both in the industrialized world and in those developing countries where natural gas is plentiful. For industrialized countries, maintaining aging nuclear power plants will be a key undertaking.

Where coal will be the principal energy resource in the electricity supply sector, the implementation of clean coal technologies is an option. The simplest of these technologies, coal washing, can remove 20 to 50 percent of the sulfur in coal at a moderate cost, making it an attractive if only partially effective option for developing countries. New combustion technologies can help reduce emissions from coal-fired installations, but their costs are considerable. Advanced burners have reduced nitrogen oxide emissions by 50 percent at some facilities. Use of fluidized bed combustion or integrated gasification/combined cycle at some new plants has resulted in substantial reductions of both sulfur dioxide and nitrogen oxide emissions. The most common technological emission fixes to date, known as scrubbers, remove pollutants from effluent gases in the smokestack. Costs are high, especially for retrofitting older facilities, but results can be impressive. While no economic technologies currently exist to remove carbon dioxide from the emissions of coal-fired plants, high-efficiency technology can cost-effectively reduce carbon dioxide emissions per unit of energy supplied.

Given the current low vehicle densities in most non-OECD countries, there is enormous potential for expansion of the world's transportation sector.[15] Directly or indirectly, the expansion of the global transportation sector will worsen the problems of urban smog (mostly ozone), acid deposition, and global climate change. There is additional substantial progress to be made with gasoline-powered vehicles in fuel-efficiency (including through the use of lighter-weight materials in constructing these vehicles) and in emissions control. Nevertheless, to mitigate the environmental consequences of an expanding transportation sector, an eventual transition will be needed away from gasoline-powered vehicles to ones powered by alternative fuels. The alternative fuels attracting the most attention now are compressed/liquefied natural gas, liquefied petroleum gas, methanol, and ethanol. The replacement of the internal combustion-powered engine will eventually be needed. Electrically-powered vehicles are viewed as the logical successor; however, unless technical breakthroughs extend the batteries' range and lower costs, they are unlikely to make an impact in the short-term. Rapid improvement in the performance of fuel cells is one development that may solve many of the limitations of electrically powered vehicles. Fuel cells would eliminate the need for massive batteries and remote power generation while increasing the range of electric vehicles to match internal combustion-powered vehicles. In addition to developing alternatively fueled vehicles, efforts should continue in improving and building more public transport infrastructure.

Wider use of renewable energy resources would dramatically reduce emissions of nearly every harmful air pollutant. At present, renewable energy does not account for a significant portion of the world's energy supply.[16] Excluding hydropower, renewables generate less than one percent of the world's electricity.

There are five renewable energy technologies that have the potential to make a significant contribution to sustainable development: (1) *Solid biomass combustion* is used for both heating and electricity. The primary sources of biomass for electricity production

---

[15]By 2010, the transport sector will account for more than 60 percent of the world's final oil consumption.

[16]According to the IEA, hydro (2.4 percent) and other renewables (.4 percent) accounted for 2.8 percent of total primary commercial energy supply in 1992. These numbers do not account for non-commercial energy like wood or dung which are widely used in some developing countries. It is estimated, for instance, that 70 percent of African energy supply is from non-commercial biomass. Non-commercial energy also plays an important role in India and China. As a percentage of world energy supply, non-commercial wood and other gathered biomass would add possibly a single percentage point to renewables' contribution.

are wood, wood wastes, and wood byproducts, but agricultural wastes and municipal solid wastes are also important sources. Biomass is a critical source of energy for many developing countries, but is generally used inefficiently. (2) *Photovoltaic cells* convert solar radiation directly into electricity. A unit of electricity generated from PVs is now far more expensive than a unit generated from fossil fuels (30-40 cents per kilowatt-hour [kWh], compared with 3-6 cents). Nevertheless, costs are coming down significantly as efficiency improves. PVs are competitive in some rural areas that are not grid-connected because their distribution costs are much lower than conventional forms of energy. This is particularly the case in developing countries where electricity grids often have not been established. (3) *Wind power* converts the kinetic energy of wind into rotational energy which drives electricity-generating turbines. There are approximately 25,000 grid-connected electricity-generating wind turbines in operation throughout the world. The cost of wind power is dropping, and in some cases is directly competitive (with no subsidies) with fossil-fuel fired power plants. For utility-scale turbines, the kWh cost dropped from $0.68 in 1980 to $0.06 by 1990. (4) *Geothermal* energy is heat trapped up to 3,000 feet below the Earth's surface. The resource can be found in four different forms, but hydrothermal is the principal form that is commercially exploited. (5) *Passive solar* uses elements of building design rather than mechanical systems to capture and store solar energy for heating, cooling, ventilation, and lighting. Depending on the region, passive solar design can provide 50 to 80 percent of building-heating requirements in the United States.

Before renewables will make a significant impact, several challenges will have to be overcome, including reducing costs, improving technologies and efficiency, enhancing reliability, solving the problem of energy storage, and integrating the technology into existing energy systems. We believe it is important for OECD governments to support basic research relating to the most promising renewable energy technologies. Public subsidies should disappear as commercialization approaches. Subsidization often impedes efforts to arrive at a competitive edge by the firms concerned.

We cannot emphasize too much that increasing energy efficiency is a cost-effective and flexible tool for addressing environmental challenges. Energy efficiency increased rapidly throughout industrialized countries in the 1970s and 1980s, but the increase has slowed over the past several years, due in large part to the removal of the incentive of expected energy price increases. Recent experience indicates that a unit of energy can be conserved for roughly half the cost of adding equivalent new capacity at a power plant, with little environmental impact.

While these technologies (on both the supply and demand side) may be helpful in addressing the environmental challenges, if they are to be overcome over the long-term (to 2050 and beyond) there will have to be a more fundamental shift in energy supply and usage patterns. We can only speculate about change over such a long period; however, there are promising technologies, any one of which could make enormous contributions to a cleaner and more cost effective energy supply for sustainable development. These include highly evolved nuclear fission systems, nuclear fusion, and hydrogen as a major energy source. Future technological breakthroughs in low-temperature superconductivity would allow storage and transportation of a large amount of electricity without loss. This will make in-phase utilization of photovoltaic and wind energy more feasible, and enable distant hydro electricity stations to supply power to industrial centers. Technologies outside the energy system, such as telecommuting, could also significantly alter our energy usage patterns.

SUMMARY OF POLICY CONCLUSIONS

A complex web of interrelated issues must be addressed in assessing the energy security challenges before the Trilateral countries in the coming years and devising policies aimed at providing reasonable assurance that energy security will be maintained. In this report we have concentrated in particular on the years out to 2010, a standard benchmark year in current forecasts and about as far into the future as meaningful quantitative forecasts can be made. For some purposes, we have looked out as far as 2050, but in a necessarily much more speculative fashion.

For policymakers in Trilateral countries, maintaining energy security has three faces. The first involves limiting the world economy's vulnerability to disruption as dependence rises on oil imports from an unstable Persian Gulf region. The second involves more broadly assuring the reasonably smooth functioning of the international energy system over time—so that supply is provided for rising demand at reasonable prices. The third face of energy security is the energy-related environmental challenge. Policymakers need to help steer the evolution of the international energy system over time to keep it within the constraints of sustainable development. The policy conclusions which follow begin with the first face of energy security and proceed to the third.

1. For any policymaker who remembers the enormous disruptions associated with the oil shocks of the 1970s, the most striking aspect of energy forecasts out to 2010 is the substantial rise in the percentage of world oil supplies coming from the Persian Gulf exporters—back to the levels of the early 1970s which helped set the stage for those earlier oil shocks.

- It is possible to imagine scenarios in which high levels of dependence will not reemerge, but policymakers cannot assume such dependence will not re-emerge. Some of these alternative scenarios are undesirable despite their energy security advantages:

slower economic growth dampening the forecasted rise in demand or sharply higher energy prices for an extended period both calling forth additional non-Gulf supplies and dampening demand. Other alternative scenarios are more broadly beneficial: further upward adjustments of non-OPEC production at existing prices or accelerated improvements in the efficiency of energy use.

- There are factors which should make such high levels of dependence on the Gulf exporters somewhat—but only somewhat—easier to manage than they were in the 1970s. The world economy is less oil-dependent now than it was then and is likely to remain so through 2010. A significant integration of interests has taken place as exporters have moved into refining and other downstream activities in other parts of the world and invested more broadly in the world economy. The oil market has become a more transparent, traditional commodity market with many more players, which should facilitate timely adjustment as circumstances change. The Arab-Israeli peace process, though still troubled, has made much progress since the October 1973 war which triggered the Arab oil embargo and brought the first oil shock.

2. The likely reemergence of such substantial dependence on Persian Gulf exporters is a serious, ongoing concern with important policy implications for Trilateral countries.

- The Trilateral countries must maintain in active working order the arrangements for coordinated responses to emergencies evolved in the framework of the IEA since the first oil shock, refining these arrangements to fit changing circumstances.
- We have learned that we must deal with emergencies in a coordinated manner. Extraordinary national efforts to secure supplies and isolate national markets from international developments tend to heighten disruption, not minimize it. This lesson is easy to forget in the midst of an emergency. The ongoing IEA process helps keep it in mind and maintain the necessary confidence that it will be respected.
- We have learned that market-based responses work better than government edicts which attempt to replace the market. The emphasis in the 1970s on demand and import restraints by government edict as the first line of defense has given way to a more flexible step-by-step process focused on coordinated stock-

draw, activating oil-sharing as appropriate, and underpinning the efficient functioning of the oil market. The main problem in an emergency is unlikely to be a profound and prolonged shortage of supply, but rather the economic (and political) disruption that an emergency can create in a global economy.

- We have learned that, while we can prepare for an emergency, we must act flexibly according to the circumstances of a particular crisis. An important element of the tailor-made response during the Gulf War was the informal and effective cooperation between the IEA Executive Director and member governments involved in the political/military activities in the Persian Gulf (including the U.S. National Security Council), which ensured a degree of integration between management of the energy emergency and the political/military actions of the U.S.-led coalition.

- The behavior of non-IEA consuming nations will become more important in emergencies as these countries constitute an increasing portion of world demand. We do not recommend the enlargement of the IEA membership in this report, but we do support reaching out to key non-member countries in the development of emergency arrangements. Rapidly growing countries in Asia, for example, could be encouraged to develop stocks, and to coordinate their stock draw and demand restraint measures with IEA countries during a crisis.

- The IEA countries should be alert to opportunities for cooperation with the oil exporters, including opportunities to advance the integration of interests in the global marketplace. Saudi Arabia, for instance, was able to provide critical surge capacity when Iraqi and Kuwaiti supplies to the market were drastically reduced during the Gulf War.

- The rise in dependence on the Gulf exporters will reinforce the importance of security in the Gulf. There are other reasons for Trilateral countries to worry about security in the Gulf region—the proliferation of weapons of mass destruction, the support of terrorism by some regimes in the region, the progress of the Arab-Israeli peace process. This is a complex mix and sometimes other objectives will cut across and subordinate energy security objectives (arguably the case in current U.S. policy toward Iran), but energy security objectives will remain part of the equation in this unstable area. While the Arab-Israeli peace process has made great steps forward since the early 1970s, some key regimes may be threatened by internal collapse and some governments may present threats to key neighbors. The security burdens in the region have been borne disproportionately by the United States, although less so than some Americans think. The Gulf War was a good demonstration of military cooperation between the United States and some European countries, and countries in the region. The Trilateral countries might have to face such a challenge again in the future. The NATO-led force (IFOR) now in Bosnia may offer another relevant example of multilateral action.

3. National energy policies of Trilateral countries will vary according to national circumstances and objectives, but in their own ways can slow the rise in dependence on the swing producers in the Persian Gulf through encouraging the development of diverse additional supplies, greater efficiency in energy use, and new energy technologies.

- Countries with slender domestic fossil fuel reserves tend to have taken stronger action to assure security of supply. Japan, which has dramatically reduced its dependence on imported oil since 1973 through a variety of measures, is the most striking case among Trilateral countries. Its energy policies have made a largely positive contribution to collective energy security. France has also made impressive progress in this area.

- Conversely, countries with great domestic fossil fuel reserves tend to feel less vulnerable and to have taken less strong national action. Energy security is a low priority concern in Canada at the moment, for instance, and Canada is without publicly held stocks, without significant surge capacity and with little room to quickly improve efficiency of energy use.

- Different countries contribute in different ways to collective energy security. The United States, for instance, maintains a 600 million barrel Strategic Petroleum Reserve and major military forces in the Gulf region, but is among the least active Trilateral countries in using increased taxes to encourage greater efficiency of energy use and production.

- Energy security measures taken by one country benefit other countries. For example, a clean coal plant in the United States or Germany, nuclear-generated electricity in France, or LNG imports in Japan all reduce the collective dependence of global energy consumers on the volatile Persian Gulf. A barrel produced or saved anywhere outside the Gulf is of benefit to all consumers in our highly interdependent, integrated global oil market.

- The IEA framework has been important in the general progress Trilateral countries have made in building more flexible energy sectors—through diversification of supplies, through deregulation and greater transparency of markets, through energy efficiency gains, and through developing new energy technologies. The IEA embarked on a long-term program in 1977 which has been adjusted over time to changing circumstances and global markets. The most recent policy update is the statement of "Shared Goals" adopted by Ministers at the June 1993 Ministerial meeting, printed as Apprendix B of this report. This needs to be a continuing effort.

4. The trend toward greater market orientation in Trilateral energy policies is positive, though still somewhat experimental. The extent of market orientation varies among countries, though the trend is in the same direction.

- Most Trilateral governments moved toward more intervention in energy markets after the first oil shock, but over time this trend has been sharply reversed. One reason for the move toward greater market orientation is that the assumptions regarding higher energy prices and limited supplies upon which the earlier government interventions were based turned out to be wrong. Governments cannot intervene against market forces for extended periods of time, and at the same time markets have provided a reasonable measure of stability in recent years.

- Policymakers should not think of reliance on market forces and assurance of energy security as opposite ends of the policy spectrum. Indeed, reliance on market forces, open trade, and a secure framework for investment are essential elements for ensuring long-term energy security. The task for policymakers is not to replace markets but rather to understand, monitor and make use of market forces in containing the disruption associated with emergencies and establishing framework conditions that encourage the healthy functioning of markets over time.

5. The continuing implementation of market-oriented reforms in Russia is critical for expanding Russia's contribution to world energy supplies and for Russia's energy resources to become a major contributor to the general welfare of the country.

- The Trilateral countries should encourage Russia to continue establishing a regulatory and legal environment more conducive to foreign investment. To date the Russian energy sector has attracted far less foreign investment than have the energy resources of Central Asia and the Caucasus.

- While the "European" character of the initial Energy Charter seemed to exclude others and there are some legal complications for the Americans and Canadians, no better multilateral tool now exists than the Energy Charter Treaty to protect foreign investment in the energy sector. Japan has signed the Treaty. We recommend that the United States and Canada do so as well.

6. The optimal outcome in Central Asia and the Caucasus will be the development of multiple pipeline routes. Multiple pipelines will not only enhance the security of these Newly Independent States and the export of their substantial energy resources to international markets, but will introduce greater competition and result in lower costs over time.

- Utilizing the framework of the Energy Charter Treaty and the International Energy Agency, we recommend that an intergovernmental study group be convened to elaborate a regime for protecting the integrity of international oil and gas transport in this and other regions.

- Pipelines through Iran to the growing markets of Asia should not be ruled out over the long-term.

7. Energy use is growing particularly strongly in the rapidly industrializing countries of Asia. The Trilateral countries, and the broad multilateral institutions in which our countries are involved, can seek to improve global energy security by participating in this economic growth in ways that serve energy security objectives. One interest shared by Trilateral countries and rapidly industrializing countries is that this growth be as energy-efficient as possible.

- The energy efficiency of the massive projected development of energy infrastructure in these countries in the coming years is important in this regard. In China, for instance, government plans call for the construction of a new power plant every month for the next ten years. There are environmental concerns associated with this infrastructure development, particularly increased burning of high-sulfur Chinese coal. The ambitious plans for expanding nuclear power in China also arouse unease in the region.

- In China and the rest of developing Asia, the combination in the coming years of vigorous growth in energy demand and increased reliance on imported oil will heighten the political importance of energy security in the region and present both challenges and opportunities for Asia-Pacific development. Natural gas, in particular, offers clean and reasonably priced energy for this rapidly growing region. It is imperative that nations of East Asia adopt clean coal technology.

8. Although the expansion of nuclear power generating capacity has dramatically slowed in North America and Europe, expansion continues in Japan and developing Asia. North America and Europe may turn back to expansion of this energy source in the period after 2010.

- We believe that problems of operating safety and long-term waste disposal are manageable, as are the proliferation risks associated with nuclear power. The framework for global cooperation provided by the International Atomic Energy Agency (IAEA) is of critical importance in these efforts. To increase assurance of the successful management of these problems and risks as nuclear power expands in developing East Asia, we support the development of regional fuel cycle arrangements including Japan.

- The improvement of safety standards and shutting down of unsafe operational reactors are critical in Russia and Ukraine and elsewhere in the former Soviet empire. The Trilateral countries should contribute generously to development of the replacement power which these countries demand be in view before unsafe reactors are shut down.

- The greatest contribution of nuclear power to energy security may be in the context of long-term sustainable development, should the growth of fossil fuel emissions need to be significantly curtailed. Trilateral countries should continue to support the reprocessing of spent nuclear fuel, which results in a more efficient use of uranium resources and reduces the overall volume of nuclear waste materials. Research and development efforts should continue on advanced nuclear reactors, including efforts by France and Japan to commercialize fast breeder technology in the next century.

9. The third face of energy security, the "sustainable development" face, will continue to be of considerable salience in the energy policy debates in our countries.

- The risks of global warming associated with rising greenhouse gas emissions are sufficient to merit sustained efforts by policymakers in Trilateral countries to find ways to moderate this rise in a market-oriented manner. There is a substantial gap between the sweeping commitments made by many Trilateral governments to stem the rise in greenhouse gas emissions in their countries and any available means for implementation.

- The projected rise of sulfur dioxide emissions in Asia in the coming years will bring increasingly serious acid deposition problems to the region. The methods used to contain and reduce these emissions in Trilateral countries in recent decades should be of some use in moderating the rise of sulfur dioxide emissions in developing Asia.

- Trilateral governments should maintain their active support of basic research into alternative technologies for producing and utilizing energy. If we raise our sights to 2050 and beyond, the world is likely to require a fundamental shift in energy supply and usage patterns, relying more on advanced clean energy systems including nuclear power and renewables. Over the longer term, it is unlikely that the United States can sustain a large military presence in the Gulf; therefore, it will be important to shift to energy systems less dependent on military and political developments. It is in the nature of basic research that we cannot predict the timing of breakthroughs, but support of this research must be sustained to allow progress to be made.

10. Maintaining energy security in a global context is a broad foreign policy challenge. It can only be accomplished by the Trilateral countries working together, providing constructive leadership which takes into account the needs of the wider international system—the underlying idea that drives the Trilateral Commission. The Trilateral countries cannot accomplish the maintenance of energy security on their own, but it will only be accomplished if the Trilateral countries provide constructive leadership for the wider effort. National energy policies of Trilateral countries will vary according to national circumstances and objectives, but can and should contribute to collective needs.

Appendices

APPENDIX A:

Energy Charter Treaty

On December 17, 1991, at a conference in The Hague, the *European Energy Charter* was signed by over fifty countries—including all members of the European Community, Central and Eastern European countries, Russia and all other states in the area of the former Soviet Union, the United States and Canada, Japan and Australia, and several others. The objectives of the Charter are to improve security of supply; to maximize the efficiency of production, conversion, transport, distribution and use of energy; to enhance safety; and to minimize environmental problems—all through applying the principles of non-discrimination and of market-oriented pricing. In the European Energy Charter, which is a declaration of political intent, the signatories undertook to negotiate a legally binding treaty and to negotiate additional protocols.

The *Energy Charter Treaty*, together with the Protocol on Energy Efficiency and Related Environment Aspects, was opened for signature on December 19, 1994. The Treaty and Protocol are expected to enter into force in 1996 after 30 signatories have ratified them. The signatories to the Energy Charter Treaty include the signatories of the European Energy Charter with the exception of the United States and Canada.

The Treaty is applicable to all economic activities related to the energy sector, from exploration at one end to marketing and sales at the other. The energy sector is broadly defined.

The Treaty stipulates that trade in energy materials and products among Contracting Parties shall be governed by the provisions of the GATT and its related instruments, including Contracting Parties not parties to the GATT. With regard to non-GATT members, the Treaty provides for the application of GATT rules *mutatis mutandis*. The Treaty thus facilitates access to markets in all the Contracting Parties.

Alongside the trade rules, the Treaty ensures transit across third countries in sending energy to export markets. The Treaty stipulates that each country concerned must take the measures necessary to facilitate such transit and, in particular, prohibits interrupting the flow of energy in the event of any dispute over the terms and conditions of transit, until an amicable solution is found or a court ruling given.

The Treaty obliges the Contracting Parties to encourage and create stable, equitable and transparent conditions for foreign investors in their countries. The Contracting Parties commit themselves to facilitate access to resources and, therefore, to rules on the exploration, development and acquisition of energy resources which are transparent and nondiscriminatory. The investment provisions of the Treaty create legally binding obligations. Each Contracting Party agrees to treat foreign investors at least as well as it treats its national or domestic companies or investors, after the pre-investment phase. In addition, the Treaty establishes international standards of treatment similar to those found in bilateral investment protection treaties.

For the pre-investment phase, the implementation of the national treatment principle will be in two stages. In the first stage, potential foreign investors will receive either national treatment or most-favored-nation treatment on a voluntary basis ("best efforts"). In the second stage (3 years after signature at the most), all signatories are committed to extend national treatment to the pre-investment phase, on a legally binding basis, subject to conditions to be defined in a supplementary treaty which is under negotiation.

The dispute settlement mechanisms, which are exceptionally well-defined and forceful compared to many other treaties, provide for final and binding resolutions of many disputes. There are separate dispute settlement procedures for disputes between states and those between states and investors.

All provisions of the Treaty will not immediately apply to all its signatories in an equal manner. Countries "in transition" that need time to adapt to the requirements of a market economy are granted transitional arrangements. Full compliance with the relevant obligations is to be in place by July 1, 2001.

Before the Treaty's entry into force, most parties have undertaken to apply it on a provisional basis as far as allowed by the signatories' constitutions, laws or regulations.

Historically, East-West relations in the investment field have been based on bilateral investment treaties. Furthermore, the EU and its member states have signed partnership and cooperation agreements with Russia and several of the other former Soviet Republics. These agreements refer to the Energy Charter Treaty as far as energy sector is concerned.

The Energy Charter Conference, established by the Treaty, is envisaged as the forum for East-West dialogue on energy issues, "encouraging cooperative efforts aimed at facilitating and promoting market-oriented reforms and modernization of energy sectors in those countries of Central and Eastern Europe and the former Union of Soviet Socialist Republics undergoing economic transition." The Energy Charter Conference is served by a Secretariat. The Secretariat, based in Brussels, has been operational since January 1, 1996.

1. Signatories of Energy Charter Treaty

Albania	Georgia	Netherlands
Armenia	Germany	Norway
Australia	Greece	Poland
Austria	Hungary	Portugal
Azerbaijan	Iceland	Romania
Belarus	Ireland	Russian Federation
Belgium	Italy	Slovakia
Bosnia Herzegovina	Japan	Slovenia
Bulgaria	Kazakhstan	Spain
Croatia	Kyrgyzstan	Sweden
Cyprus	Latvia	Switzerland
Czech Republic	Liechtenstein	Tajikistan
Denmark	Lithuania	Turkey
Estonia	Luxembourg	Turkmenistan
Finland	Malta	Ukraine
France	Moldova	United Kingdom
		Uzbekistan
		European Union

2. Signatories of European Energy Charter, but not of
   Energy Charter Treaty

Canada   United States

3. Observers at Energy Charter Conference

Algeria	Bahrain	Venezuela
Kuwait	Morocco	Oman
Qatar	Saudi Arabia	Tunisia
United Arab Emirates		

APPENDIX B:

Shared Goals
International Energy Agency
Statement of Ministers, June 1993

The 23 member countries of the International Energy Agency (IEA) seek to create the conditions in which the energy sectors of their economies can make the fullest possible contribution to sustainable economic development and the well-being of their people and of the environment. In formulating energy policies, the establishment of free and open markets is a fundamental point of departure, though energy security and environmental protection need to be given particular emphasis by governments. IEA countries recognize the significance of increasing global interdependence in energy. They therefore seek to promote the effective operation of international energy markets and encourage dialogue with all participants. In order to secure their objectives they therefore aim to create a policy framework consistent with the following goals.[1]

1. Diversity, efficiency and flexibility within the energy sector are basic conditions for longer-term energy security; the fuels used within and across sectors and the sources of those fuels should be as diverse as practicable. Non fossil-fuels, particularly nuclear and hydro-power, make a substantial contribution to the energy supply diversity of IEA countries as a group.

2. Energy systems should have the ability to respond promptly and flexibly to energy emergencies. In some cases this requires collective mechanisms and action—IEA countries' cooperation through the Agency in responding jointly to oil supply emergencies.

3. The environmentally sustainable provision and use of energy is central to the achievement of these shared goals. Decision-makers should seek to minimize the adverse environmental impacts of energy activities, just as the environmental decisions should take account of the energy consequences. Government interventions should, where practicable, have regard to the Polluter Pays Principle.

4. More environmentally acceptable energy sources need to be encouraged and developed. Clean and efficient use of fossil fuels is essential. The development of economic non-fossil sources is also a priority. A number of IEA members wish to retain and improve the nuclear option for the future, at the highest available safety standards, because nuclear energy does not emit carbon dioxide. Renewable sources will also have an increasingly important contribution to make.

---

[1] IEA member countries include: Australia, Austria, Belgium, Canada, Denmark, Finland, France, Germany, Greece, Ireland, Italy, Japan, Luxembourg, Netherlands, New Zealand, Norway, Portugal, Spain, Sweden, Switzerland, Turkey, United Kingdom, and the United States. The "Shared Goals" were adopted by IEA Ministers at their June 4, 1993, meeting in Paris.

5. Improved energy efficiency can promote both environmental protection and energy security in a cost-effective manner. There are significant opportunities for greater energy efficiency at all stages of the energy cycle from production to consumption. Strong efforts by governments and all energy users are needed to realize these opportunities.

6. Continued research, development and market deployment of new and improved energy technologies make a critical contribution to achieving the objectives outlined above. Energy technology policies should complement broader energy polices. International cooperation in the development and dissemination of energy technologies, including industry participation and co-operation with non-Member countries, should be encouraged.

7. Undistorted energy prices enable markets to work efficiently. Energy prices should not be held artificially below the costs of supply to promote social or industrial goals. To the extent necessary and practicable, the environmental cost of energy production should be reflected in prices.

8. Free and open trade and a secure framework for investment contribute to efficient energy markets and energy security. Distortions to energy trade and investment should be avoided.

9. Cooperation among all energy market participants helps to improve information and understanding, and encourage the development of efficient, environmentally acceptable and flexible energy systems and markets worldwide. These are needed to help promote the investment, trade and confidence necessary to achieve global energy security and environmental objectives.

APPENDIX C:
Description of the GEMS
Global Energy Supply and Demand Model

The GEMS Global Energy Supply and Demand Model generates energy supply and demand projections for major countries, regions and the world as a whole for the years 2000 and 2010. For this presentation, GEMS has developed two scenarios: (1) "business as usual," and (2) "energy security." Under the "business as usual" scenario, projections are based on current practices that rely heavily on oil for transportation and coal for electrification. The "energy security" scenario incorporates reduced dependence on oil and coal; lower energy intensity; support for domestic sources of energy such as oil, gas, and nuclear power; and increased diversity of energy shares in electricity generation and transportation. In this second scenario, heavy reliance on Persian Gulf oil is be reduced.

Countries and Regions

The GEMS Model compiles energy statistics from the base year 1990[1] to develop energy demand projections for Canada, China, France, Germany, India, Japan, South Korea, Taiwan, the United Kingdom, and the United States. These projections are incorporated into the regional statistics compiled for Africa, the former Soviet Union, Latin America, the Middle East, Non-OECD Asia, Non-OECD Europe, OECD Europe, OECD North America, OECD Pacific and the OECD Total. The regional totals are aggregated in the world total.[2] GEMS uses the standard energy supply/demand integration sheet used extensively by energy analysts around the world.

Assumptions

The assumptions made for each country and region include economic growth, energy/GDP ratios, oil price, indigenous production estimates, and sector demand shares.

•*Economic growth:* The economic growth assumptions are calculated from data available from the OECD Secretariat and the World Bank. The average economic growth rate for OECD countries is projected to be approximately 2.3 percent out to 2010. In rapidly developing countries the economic growth rate is much higher, with an average of 5.3 percent out to 2010.

---

[1]All projections are made from base-year statistics for 1990, compiled from IEA publications: *Energy Statistics and Balances of Non-OECD Countries 1989-1990* (Paris) and *Energy Balances of OECD Countries 1990-1991* (Paris).
[2]China is not included in Non-OECD Asia. China is added to the regional totals in the compilation of the world total.

•*Energy /GDP Ratio:* The energy/GDP ratio is one of the most important assumptions made in the model. This ratio determines the energy intensity of a country and makes the distinction between rapidly industrializing (China and India) and industrialized (OECD) countries. Rapidly industrializing countries have a higher energy/GDP ratio because their industries (steel and heavy manufacturing) are more energy intensive. Industrialized countries have lower energy/GDP ratios because their industries (service industries) are less energy intensive. This ratio is multiplied by the economic growth rate to determine the final energy demand growth rate. The GEMS Model takes into account that the energy efficiency of technologies used by developing countries is steadily improving. While they may not always adopt the most efficient technologies, the basic standard has risen dramatically over the last 15 to 20 years, allowing developing countries to leap-frog to more efficient energy technologies. Having the benefit of more efficient technologies will result in developing countries having lower energy/GDP ratios than currently industrialized countries at a similar earlier stage of development.

•*Oil Price:* The price of oil is assumed to rise from $18 per barrel in 1995 to $24 per barrel in 2010 in 1995 U.S. dollars. Oil markets are thus expected to remain steady over the period.

•*Indigenous Production Estimates*: GEMS estimates country and regional indigenous energy production (oil, coal, and natural gas) based on figures from the OECD, the U.S. Department of Energy, and the World Bank.

•*Sector Demand Shares:* The sector demand shares by fuel for the transportation, industrial, and commercial/residential sectors are based on the 1990 base year data. For the different scenarios, changes are made to the sector demand shares to show increased (or decreased) usage of oil, coal, natural gas, nuclear, and renewable energy sources in each sector over the twenty-year period to 2010.

"Business as Usual" Scenario

Assumptions made in the "business as usual" scenario include higher energy/GDP ratios; lower prices of fossil fuels; continued dependence on oil for transportation and on coal for electricity production; and an increase in the use of petroleum for electricity production. The largest growth in oil production to meet world demand comes from the Persian Gulf, which contains over 60 percent of known world oil reserves. Even with only a moderate decline of OECD oil production, the Persian Gulf will have to increase its oil production capacity by nearly 100 percent to meet the projected world demand in 2010.

"Energy Security" Scenario

In the "energy security" scenario, GEMS takes into account environmental concerns and economic competitiveness. Assumptions include lower energy /GDP ratios due to greater energy efficiency; increased electrification of the transportation sector; government policies that increase the use of natural gas and nuclear power; and greater conservation efforts.

FIGURE 18

Comparison of GEMS Scenarios

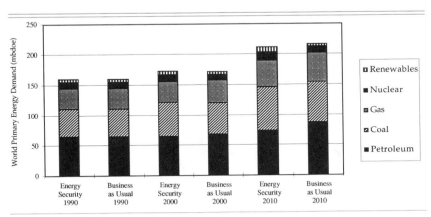

Source: GEMS Global Energy Supply and Demand Model

The increased diversity of energy sources results in a remarkable difference in the world demand for oil. Under this scenario, world oil demand would be 8.4 mb/d less than under the "business as usual" scenario by 2010. These are 8.4 mb/d of oil that will not have to be produced in the Persian Gulf. In this scenario, Persian Gulf oil production capacity would only have to increase by 54 percent to meet world demand. World carbon dioxide emissions in 2010 would also be reduced by about 20 percent from the "business as usual" scenario.